OECD Reviews of Health Systems: Colombia 2016

OECD
BETTER POLICIES FOR BETTER LIVES

Please cite this publication as:
OECD (2015), *OECD Reviews of Health Systems: Colombia 2016*, OECD Publishing, Paris.
http://dx.doi.org/10.1787/9789264248908-en

ISBN 978-92-64-17904-2 (print)
ISBN 978-92-64-24890-8 (PDF)

Series: OECD Reviews of Health Systems
ISSN 1990-1429 (print)
ISSN 1990-1410 (online)

Photo credits: Cover © Tomi/PhotoLink/Photodisc/Getty Images

Corrigenda to OECD publications may be found on line at: *www.oecd.org/about/publishing/corrigenda.htm*.

Foreword

Colombia's record in extending health insurance and health services to its population is impressive. In 1990, around one in six of the population had health insurance. Now, nearly 97% do, with greatest expansion occurring amongst poorer households. Likewise, in 1993 out-of-pocket spending made up 52% of total national expenditure on health. By 2006, this had fallen to less than 15% (and remains low). Although Colombia has high rates of income inequality (with a Gini coefficient of 53.5 in 2012, compared to the OECD average of 32.2), access to health care services is much more equal. In urban populations, for example, 1.8% of children aged less than two years of age are recorded as having received no routine vaccinations, compared to 1.0% of rural children.

Colombia nevertheless faces important challenges to maintain and improve the performance of its health system. Financial sustainability is a particular concern that will need concerted action now if Colombia is to maintain its ambition of universal, high-quality health care: control around the prices paid for services and around the volumes of services delivered are weak, a strategic approach to capital planning is lacking and fee-for-service payments dominate. There are a number of steps that Colombia could take to strengthen health system performance and sustainability. Key amongst them will be to ensure that the health insurers ("*entidades promotoras de salud*") evolve into effective and efficient purchasers of care, understanding population health care needs, engaging in prevention and early detection, and awarding contracts to providers based on robust measures of quality and outcomes.

This document consists of a background report prepared by the OECD Secretariat to support the Health System Review of Colombia which is currently being undertaken by the OECD Health Committee as part of the process for Colombia's accession to the OECD (see the Roadmap for the Accession of Colombia to the OECD Convention [C(2013)110/FINAL]).

In accordance with paragraph 14 of Colombia's Accession Roadmap, the Health Committee agreed to declassify the report in its current version and publish it under the authority of the Secretary General, in order to allow a wider audience to become acquainted with the issues raised in the report. Publication of this document and the analysis and recommendations contained therein, does not prejudge in any way the results of the ongoing review of Colombia by the Health Committee as part of its process of accession to the OECD.

ACKNOWLEDGEMENTS

The lead author of this Health System Review was Ian Forde. The other authors of this report were Rodrigo Moreno-Serra, Geronimo Salomón Holmer and Alejandro Posada. Oscar Bernal, Carlos Grijalba and Maria Luisa Latorre also authored material for Chapter 1. The authors wish to thank Francesca Colombo, Mark Pearson and Stefano Scarpetta from the OECD Directorate of Employment, Labour and Social Affairs for their comments and suggestions. Thanks also go to Marlène Mohier and Lucy Hulett for their editorial input and to Duniya Dedyn, Susannah Nash and Judy Zinnemann for their logistical assistance.

The completion of this report would not have been possible without the generous support of Colombian authorities. This report has benefited from the expertise and material received from many health officials, health professionals, patient groups and other health experts that the OECD Review team met during a mission to Colombia in February 2015. These included Directors at the Ministry of Health and Social Protection; Secretaries of Health in the Guanía, Cundinamarca and Bogotá regions; representatives of the Asociación Colombiana de Hospitales y Clinicas, Asociación Colombiana de Empresas Sociales del Estado y Hospitales Públicos, Fundación Santa Fé, Hospital Universitario Mayor, Hospital Pablo VI Bosa, Hospital Nazaret, Instituto de Ortopedia Infantil Roosevelt, Hospital Occidental de Kennedy, Instituto Nacional de Cancerología, Fundación Cardioinfantil, and the Fundación Cardiovascular de Colombia; representatives of the Asociación Colombiana de Empresas de Medicina Integral, Gestarsalud, Salud Total, Aliansalud, Famisanar, Compensar and SURA; representatives of the Colegio Médico Colombiano, Federación Médica Colombiana, Asociación Médica Sindical Colombiana, Asociación Colombiana de Facultades y Escuelas de Enfermería, Asociación Colombiana de Sociedades Científicas, and the Asociación Colombiana de Facultades de Medicina; representatives of Asocajas, Asociación de Industrias Farmacéuticas Colombianas, Asociación de Laboratorios Farmacéuticos de Investigación y Desarrollo, Cámara Salud Andi, Cámara de la Industria Farmacéutica Andi and the Cámara de Gases Industriales y Medicinales Andi; representatives of Pacientes Colombia, Liga Colombiana de Hemofílicos Liga Colombiana Contra el Cáncer, Liga Nacional Antituberculosa, Observatorio Interinstitucional de Cáncer de Adultos, Observatorio Interinstitucional de Cáncer de Niños, Fundación Simmon, Fundación Colombiana Fibrosis Quística, and the Comité de Veeduría Ciudadana en Salud; representatives of the World Bank, Inter-American Development Bank, Pan-American Health Organization, UNICEF, United Nations Population Fund, UN Food and Agriculture Organization and Médicos Sin Fronteras; Carlos Palacio Acosta, Fabio Bolívar, Enrique Peñaloza, David Bardey and Yuri Takeuchi Tan. Particular thanks are extended to Jorge Iván Palacios, President of the Constitutional Court for valuable discussions around the judicialisation of health care in Colombia; and to Alma Solano Sanchez and her team for a very enjoyable and informative visit to see local health services in Barranquilla.

The review team is especially thankful to Minister Alejandro Gaviria Uribe, Vice-Minister Fernando Ruiz Gómez, Vice-Minister Carmen Eugenia Dávila and their officials at the Ministry of Health and Social Protection, especially Mery Bolivar, Camilo Sanchez Meertens, Jaime Matute Hernandez and María Carmela Julio, for their support for this Review and their help with setting up the visit of OECD officials to Colombia. This report has benefited from the comments of the Colombian authorities and experts who reviewed earlier drafts.

Table of contents

Tables

Figures

Acronyms and abbreviations

APS	*Atención Primaria en Salud*	Primary care services
CAC	*Cuenta de Alto Costo*	High-cost fund
COP		Colombian peso
DALY		Disability-adjusted life year
DANE	*Departamento Administrativo Nacional de Estadística*	National Statistics Authority
DRG		Diagnosis related group
ENSIN	*Encuesta Nacional de Situación Nutricional*	National nutrition survey
EPS	*Entidad Promotora de Salud*	Health insurance agency
ET	*Entidad Territorial*	Local government authority
GDP		Gross domestic product
IPS	*Institución Prestadora de Servicios de Salud*	Health care provider
MSPS	*Ministerio de Salud y Protección Social*	Ministry of Health and Social Protection
NCD		Non-communicable disease
OCADER	*Observatorio de Salud Cardiovascular, Diabetes y Enfermedad Renal Crónica*	Observatory for Cardiovascular Health, Diabetes and Chronic Renal Disease
PDSP	*Plan Decenal de Salud Pública*	Ten-year public health plan
PEDT	*Protección Específica y Detección Temprana*	Prevention and early detection programme
POS	*Plan Obligatorio de Salud*	Basic benefits basket/package
PPP		Purchasing power parity
QOF		Quality and Outcomes Framework
REPS	*Registro Especial de Prestadores de Servicios de Salud*	Register of health care providers
RIPS	*Registro Individual de Prestaciones de Salud*	Database of services provided to individuals

SGSSS	*Sistema General de Seguridad Social en Salud*	National health system
SIG	*Sistema de Información Geográfica*	Geographic information system
SIHO	*Sistema de Información de Hospitales*	Hospital information system
SISBEN	*Sistema de Identificación de Beneficiarios de programas sociales*	System for determining individuals' eligibility for social programmes
SISPRO	*Sistema Integral de Información de la Protección Social*	Health and social care national information system
SNS	*Superintendencia Nacional de Salud*	National health inspectorate
SOGC	*Sistema Obligatorio de Garantía de Calidad de la Atención en Salud*	Quality assurance system
SUA	*Sistema Único de Acreditación*	Health care provider accreditation system
UHC		Universal Health Coverage
UPC	*Unidad de Pago por Capitación*	Per-capita allocation to EPS
WHO		World Health Organization
YLD		Years lost to disability

Executive summary

Colombia offers a remarkable example of rapid progress toward universal health coverage that deserves to be better known internationally. It has achieved financial protection against excessive health care costs for almost all citizens, as well as an equal basket of services for those in and out of formal employment. Insurance coverage has risen rapidly from 23.5% of the population in 1993 to 96.6% in 2014. Affiliation increased most rapidly in the poorest quintiles (from 4.3% in 1993 to 89.3% in 2013) and in rural areas (from 6.6% in 1993 to 92.6% in 2013). Likewise, in 1993 out-of-pocket spending made up 52% of total national expenditure on health. By 2006, this had fallen to less than 15%, and remains one of the lowest figures in the region.

Improvements in health coverage is demonstrated in some key metrics, such as reductions in unmet health needs, reductions in waiting times for an appointment, increased preventive health care consultations and increased perceptions of quality by service users. As with the extension of financial protection, improved access to services has mostly benefited the poorest Colombians: reported unmet health care needs in the past month fell from 33.2% of those surveyed in 1993 to 2.0% in 2013 (compared to 7.3% and 0.9% respectively amongst the richest quintile) and preventive health care consultations (in the 12 months prior to being surveyed) rose from 30.1% of the population surveyed in 1993 to 62.8% in 2010 (compared to 50.2% and 78.9% respectively amongst the richest quintile).

Despite these achievements, the Colombian health sector faces important challenges to maintain and improve efficiency and sustainability. The envisaged model of managed competition between payers, for example, has not convincingly materialised in practice, resulting in weak incentives quality and cost at the provider level. A primary goal must be to ensure that the insurers and purchasers of care (*Entidades Promotoras de Salud*, EPS) evolve into effective and efficient purchasers of care, understanding population health care needs, engaging in prevention and early detection, and awarding contracts to providers based on robust measures of quality and outcomes.

EPS are key institutions that should manage both clinical risk (through effective prevention, early diagnosis and quality-management of health care providers) and financial risk (by managing demand, and contracting intelligently with providers and suppliers). Too often, however, EPS act as mere financial clearing houses, lacking effective engagement with either consumers or providers. Greater accountability for the role of EPS in improving population health outcomes, quality of care, financial sustainability and good governance is needed. The Colombian authorities should also identify how international best practice in risk-adjustment mechanisms can be applied to EPS. Several OECD countries have developed sophisticated risk-adjustment formulae which can be used to ensure that EPS are adequately resourced for their affiliated population, whilst providing incentives to control spending.

Colombia should also work towards developing a stronger performance management framework around clinics, hospitals and other health care providers. *Atención Primaria en Salud* (APS), Colombia's primary care system, is rightly seen as fundamental to meeting population health care needs. The health system benefits a clear hierarchy of service levels, with the primary level serving as the main point of entry into the health system for patients, with the exception of emergency services. Reforms in 2012 sought to improve prevention and early detection of certain conditions such as cervical and breast cancer, or problems in childhood development, through a programme known as *Protección Específica y Detección Temprana* (PEDT) and the *Politica de Atención Integral en Salud* (PAIS, or integrated health care policy) is a new model of care that aims to better integrate primary care, public health activities and wider intersectoral action at community level.

Despite this ambitious policy programme, implementation can be hampered because health care providers are not fulfilling their potential. The Ministry of Health has set out an expectation that 90% of consultations should be resolved at the primary care level, without the need for referral to secondary care. But poor employment contracts, inefficient payment systems and a lack of quality-related infrastructure mean that this sector is not performing as well as it should. Payment systems should evolve to increasingly reward quality and outcomes, rather than activity, in both primary care and secondary care. Colombia should look to international best practice in risk-adjustment mechanisms to understand how providers can best be reimbursed in a way that allows them to meet local population health care needs, whilst containing costs. Colombia should also create a specialist primary care workforce, focused on preventing and managing chronic conditions such as diabetes. This should be underpinned by a more extensive set of primary care standards and guidelines and a specialist training curriculum.

Finally, steps should be taken to ensure that health system information is used as effectively as possible to drive continuous quality and efficiency gains. Colombia has started to build a sophisticated information infrastructure to monitor health care activities, costs and quality. SISPRO (*Sistema Integral de Información de la Protección Social*) is a data warehouse that is intended to bring together several databases that cover financing and health accounts; individuals' health care needs, risk factors and service utilisation; distribution and characteristics of insurers; and, distribution and characteristics of providers, including some indicators of quality and outcomes. Once fully operational, SISPRO will support health system monitoring and planning, as well as providing public access to key health system statistics and reports. Its website (www.sispro.gov.co) already allows users to construct search queries on insurance coverage, service use and high-level outcomes such as mortality. More detailed information on service quality and outcomes is lacking, however.

Colombia should extend its participation in international benchmarking efforts for health system quality and efficiency. In particular, increased effort is needed to submit valid and comparable data to OECD frameworks such as the *System of Health Accounts* and *Health Care Quality Indicators*. Benchmarking itself against OECD health systems will be a vital tool in helping Colombia realise continued quality and efficiency gains in its health system. Given the country's impressive achievements in reaching universal health coverage both rapidly and equitably, and in developing key institutions and ambitious policy programmes to improve population health, Colombia's greater participation in OECD activities will also bring significant benefit to the international community.

Assessment and recommendations

Colombia has a well-designed health system, with broadly effective policies and institutions that other countries could learn from and that deserves to be better known internationally. Colombia has achieved financial protection against excessive health care costs for almost all citizens, as well as an equal basket of services for those in and out of formal employment. Insurance coverage has risen rapidly from 23.5% of the population in 1993 to 96.6% in 2014, with individual's out-of-pocket spending on health care falling from 52% in 1993 to 14.4% of total national spend on health in 2013, one of the lowest figures in the region. Per capita allocation of funds for health care is equal for those in contributory and publicly-subsidised insurance schemes. Annual consumption of health care for those enrolled in contributory schemes, however, appears less equal at USD PPP 834 per year (2013), compared to USD PPP 449 for those enrolled in publicly-subsidised insurance (although the former figure includes transaction costs). Population health parameters are improving rapidly: life expectancy is now 72.1 years for men and 78.5 years for women (2013), around four years less than OECD averages, and infant mortality has fallen from 40 deaths per 1 000 live births (1970) to 12.8 in 2013 (OECD average 4.1).

The country also demonstrates capable health system governance and effective policy making: Law 100 of 1993 was an ambitious and comprehensive structural reform that introduced a purchaser-provider split, managed competition and consumer choice (of both insurers and providers). Despite significant unanticipated difficulties (such as a sharp economic contraction at the end of the 1990s) and a degree of sustained opposition to reform programme (principally against the introduction of market mechanisms into health care provision), reforms have been maintained and strengthened over the past 20 years. Subsequent legislation has sought to strengthen primary care and rural and remote care in particular. Such progress has allowed Colombia to become a regional leader in key activities. Its health technology assessment agency, *Instituto de Evaluación Tecnológica en Salud*, is one of the most advanced in Latin America, for example.

Considerable resources have also been targeted towards dealing with the legacy of Colombia's long-standing internal conflict. The conflict has led to displacement and forced possession of land, forced recruitment and kidnapping, homicides, injuries and sexual violence. In total, 7.1 million are estimated to have been victims of the armed conflict between 1985 and 2015 – mostly rural, impoverished Colombians. Colombia has halved its homicide rate, which now stands at 28 per 100 000 inhabitants (although this remains much higher than the OECD average of four homicides per 100 000 inhabitants). Nevertheless, 6.4 million people are registered as displaced as a consequence of the conflict – one of the highest national figures in the world. Steps towards building a post-conflict society are underway, one of which is the *Programa de Atención Psicosocial a Víctimas de la Violencia.* This is a EUR 670 million (USD 737 million) programme that aims to offer individually-tailored psychosocial and medical care to 3.7 million victims of the conflict, structured over four years. Thirty regional round-tables were held with victims of the conflict, to ensure that the programme best matched their needs, and additional resources directed to support the rehabilitation/social inclusion of individuals most heavily affected.

There are, nevertheless, several opportunities to strengthen key functions and improve health system performance. Not enough value is got out of, or demonstrated by, Colombia's *Entidades Promotoras de Salud* (EPS). These are the agencies that individuals, both in and out of formal employment, choose as insurers. They are key institutions that should manage both clinical risk (through effective prevention, early diagnosis and quality-management of health care providers) and financial risk (by managing demand, and contracting intelligently with providers and suppliers). Too often, however, they act as mere financial clearing-houses, lacking effective engagement with either consumers or providers. Primary care providers (APS), too, are not fulfilling their full potential. Colombia sees APS services as being front and centre of its health system, particularly in the struggle against the surge of chronic illnesses (such as diabetes) that the country is facing. But poor employment contracts, inefficient payment systems that reward activity and not outcomes, and a lack of quality-related infrastructure, mean that this sector is not performing as well as it should.

Financial sustainability is a particular concern that will need concerted action if Colombia is to maintain its ambition of universal, high-quality health care. Total national spend on health has increased from 5.4% GDP in 2004 to 6.8% in 2013 (equivalent to USD PPP 930 per capita). A number of observations suggest significant upward financial pressure, which is unlikely to translate into better services, in the coming years: control around the prices paid for services and around the volumes of services delivered are weak, a strategic approach to capital planning is lacking, fee-for-service payments dominate and EPS lack strong negotiating powers. Additionally, an unusual feature of the Colombian setting is the extent to which health care delivery is dictated by the Constitutional Court. Individuals petition the Court (via a "*tutela*") for treatments outside the guaranteed basket of services. In 81% of cases the Court approves these at the first hearing. The number of *tutelas* has climbed rapidly, from 24 843 in 2000 to 117 746 in 2014, at an estimated cumulative cost of USD 14 billion between 2005 and 2014. In 2012, the Constitutional Court also ruled that the benefits baskets for those in and out of formal employment should be equalised, setting a deadline of a year to achieve this. Whilst the intentions behind such rulings are no doubt sound, they significantly disrupt the Ministry of Health and Social Protection's (*Ministerio de Salud y Protección Social*, MSPS) capacity to plan.

To strengthen health system performance and sustainability, key actions that the Colombian authorities should prioritise in the coming years include:

- Developing more demanding and transparent performance frameworks around insurers (EPS), providers (IPS) and territorial authorities responsible for public health, focussed on population health outcomes, quality of care, financial sustainability and good governance.
- Drawing upon international experience to modify payment systems (to insurers, providers and the workforce) to reward quality and outcomes, rather than activity, in both primary care and secondary care. Piloting of prospective, patient-based reimbursement mechanisms over complete pathways of care, such as the DRG system used in other OECD countries, should begin.
- Developing a specialist primary care workforce, focused on preventing and managing chronic conditions such as diabetes. This should be underpinned by a more extensive set of primary care standards and guidelines and a specialist training curriculum.

- Extending Colombia's participation in international benchmarking efforts for health system quality and efficiency. In particular, increased effort is needed to submit valid and comparable data to OECD frameworks such as the *System of Health Accounts or Health Care Quality Indicators*.

Colombia's health care needs and health care system

Colombia, the fourth largest country in Latin America, is an extremely heterogeneous country both geographically and demographically. Most of Colombia's 47 million inhabitants live in the mountainous regions in the west of the country or along the Caribbean coast, with fewer in the plains and rainforest to the south and east. Urbanisation is happening rapidly. In 2014, 76.3% of the population lived in cities; by 2050 this figure is projected to reach almost 85%. The majority of Colombians are of Caucasian descent, although Afro-Colombian groups represent 10.3% of the population (nearly 4.3 million individuals) and indigenous groups (located mainly in the Amazon, Andean, Orinoquía and the Caribbean regions) represent 3.4% of the population (1.4 million individuals). The Roma people constitute another, yet smaller, minority.

Mortality rates decreased from 442 deaths per 100 000 inhabitants in 2005 to 425 in 2011. At the same time, fertility rates have been falling. In 2012 it was estimated that the global fertility rate in Colombia was 2.3 children per woman (in rural areas this figure was 2.8 children per woman). As a result, Colombia's shifting population pyramid resembles that of OECD economies, with a narrowing base and expanding numbers of older adults.

Colombia has maintained stable economic growth over the last decade. Between 2003 and 2008, GDP grew by 3.9% per year, slowing slightly to 2.7% per year between 2008 and 2013, reaching the equivalent of USD 12 695 per capita in 2013. Colombia has one of the highest inequality levels in Latin America, however, significantly surpassing OECD averages. Colombia's Gini coefficient was 53.5 in 2012 (compared to an OECD average of 32.2), although this has been falling (World Bank, 2015). Regional inequality is also a persistent problem. In departments such as Cordoba and La Guajira, for example, less than half the population live in adequate housing, compared to 90% nationally. Drinking water plants are present only in 56% of rural areas and water treatment plants in only 12% of these areas. Broadly, however, the percentage of the population with unmet basic needs has decreased and now stands at 37% across the country.

Like most emerging economies, Colombia is characterised by a high incidence of informal employment, estimated to represent around 60% of the workforce. Informality tends to be concentrated among low-skilled workers, workers aged over 55 and in rural areas. Formal jobs tend to pay nearly three times more, on average, than informal ones and the gap has been widening in recent years due to a steady growth of formal sector earnings.

Inevitably, Colombia's internal armed conflict, which has lasted for over 40 years, is highly relevant in any discussion of the country's health and health care needs. The conflict has led to displacement and forced possession of land, forced recruitment and kidnapping, homicides, injuries and sexual violence. With most victims coming from rural areas, the internal armed conflict has aggravated geographical health inequalities, not only because of direct health effects but also because of worsened access to health care, education, drinking water and transportation, as well as the stigmatisation of the population on both sides of the conflict. With 6.4 million people registered as being displaced as a consequence of the conflict between 1985 and 2015 (in addition to displaced people not registered), Colombia is included as one of the countries with the highest number of internally displaced people in the world. In total, 7.1 million are estimated to have been victims of the armed conflict between 1985 and 2015. More fortunately, over the past decade Colombia has halved its homicide rate, which now stands at 28 per 100 000 inhabitants. Nevertheless, homicide rates remain very high compared to the OECD average of four homicides per 100 000 inhabitants.

Colombia's major health care needs stem from chronic illnesses such as cardiovascular disease and cancer

Colombia and other countries in the Latin American region have often been described as having a "triple burden of disease". Of the total burden of disease in Colombia, estimated at 28 015 Disability Adjusted Life Years (DALYs) per 100 000 inhabitants in 2010 (IHME, 2014), non-communicable diseases accounted for 83%; injuries for further 8% and communicable, maternal, perinatal and nutritional conditions for 9% (Javeriana, 2014). These figures show a substantial shift from 2005, when there was a larger share of communicable diseases (15%), and a lower share of non-communicable diseases (76%). Hence, Colombia has experienced a rapid epidemiologic transition towards non-communicable diseases, with cancer and cardiovascular diseases accounting for the greatest disease burden.

Risk factors for non-communicable disease are also prevalent, although in some cases less prevalent than in the majority of OECD countries. 35% of Colombian women (aged 18 to 64 years) and 34.1% men are overweight; and 20.1% women and 11.5% men are obese (compared to 17.9% women and 17.4% men obese on average in the OECD). 19.5% Colombian men and 7.4% women are daily smokers, significantly lower than the OECD averages of 25.8% men and 16.6% women. Total alcohol consumption in Colombia was 4.4 litres per capita (15 years and older) in 2013, which is only half of the OECD average of 8.8 litres per capita. Nevertheless, 11.1% of the Colombian population (12 to 65 years of age) present a high-risk of harmful alcohol consumption, equivalent to 2.5 million people.

Mental illness deserves special mention. Unipolar major depression accounted for 37.8 and 68.8 DALYs per 1 000 men and women respectively in 2012 – and has risen above diarrhoeal diseases, respiratory infections and birth complication to become the third most important cause of DALYs in Colombia (IHME, 2014).

Significant challenges around infectious disease control and maternal and child health, however, persist. Coverage of routine childhood vaccinations in the country is 85%, but regions such as San Andres and Caldas report less than 65% coverage, again exposing important differences by geographic area. Low birth weight was ranked sixth by leading causes of burden of disease in 2005 (11 218 DALYs).

Despite these challenges, Colombians' perception of their health status has improved. According to the national health survey 2007, 16% of the population (6 to 69 years) considered their health "very good", 56.2% "good", 25.4% "average", and 2.2% "bad or very bad". Within the low income population, perceived health status as "very good" or "good" rose from 58.6% in 1997 to 74.4% in 2010. This sizeable increase may in part be related to the extension of health insurance and health care services, as described next.

Sustained, ambitious reforms have sought to create an efficient, equitable and sustainable national health system

Colombia's health system redesign of 1993 demonstrated far-sighted ambition to create an equitable, efficient and sustainable health system. Health insurance and health care services in Colombia were historically provided by a fragmented, poorly regulated set of social security institutes and private enterprises, largely benefitting wealthier Colombians. Health coverage only extended to 24% of the population and was highly unequal: while 47% of the richest quintile had health system coverage, only 4.3% in the poorest quintile enjoyed financial protection from excessive health expenditure. This system came with other problems such as a lack of health coverage for family members and exclusion of individuals with pre-existing health conditions.

In 1993, Law 100 brought about far-reaching reforms by creating the *Sistema General de Seguridad Social en Salud* (SGSSS, or General System of Social Security in Health). This was a big-bang reform that created a national health system by making health insurance mandatory for all those who could afford it, creating a single national pool for insurance contributions, splitting the purchaser and provider functions, and encouraging competition by allowing individuals to choose their insurer, and allowing insurers to selectively contract with providers. Responsibility for managing the financing and operation of health services was devolved locally, whilst steering and regulatory functions were retained and strengthened centrally, through the creation of new institutions. Crucially, under Law 100 health care became a legally enshrined right of citizens, rather than a service dependent on charitable supply.

Individuals become affiliated with the SGSSS through three regimes, namely the contributory regime (CR) for individuals in formal employment, the subsidised regime (SR) for individuals not in formal employment (which historically offered a less generous basket of services than the CR), and the much smaller Special Benefit Regime which includes the armed forces, teachers, and a state-owned petroleum company. Risk-equalisation and cross-subsidy exists both within and across the CR and SR, supporting efficiency and social solidarity. In the CR, employees pay 4% of their income and the employer 8.5% to a fund called the *Fondo de Seguridad y Garantia* (FOSYGA). Private insurance accounts for approximately one million individuals and has not increased significantly in the last five years.

Colombia has come close to achieving UHC both in terms of financial protection and access to services

Health insurance coverage now reaches 96% of the population, a rapid increase from a baseline of 24% at the inception of Law 100. These impressive gains are in large part due to new affiliations in the subsidised regime. Those drafting Law 100 assumed economic growth similar to the 1990s, equivalent to 5.1% annually, and anticipated around one-third of the population being included in the CR with a similar number in the SR. These assumptions had to be abandoned in 1999, however, when the economy suffered its biggest recession in many decades with a contraction of 4.1%. Rates of unemployment and participation in the informal labour market increased. Nevertheless, rather than abandoning the principles underlying Law 100, an explicit progressive decision was taken to accelerate enrolment in the SR in the early 2000s, as shown in the following chapter. More recently, the balance of new enrolments has tipped toward the CR. During 2014, there were 830 000 new enrolees to the system, of whom 73% were in the CR.

Individuals affiliated to the SGSSS are entitled to a package of health care services called the *Plan Obligatorio de Salud* (POS, or mandatory health plan). The POS is largely an explicit list of inclusions, determined on the basis of prevalent epidemiology and the cost-effectiveness, acceptability and safety of an intervention. Initially, the POS comprised different packages for the CR and SR, with more generous benefits in the former. Entitlements across the two are now equal, in theory. But as signalled by the rapid rise in appeals to the Constitutional Court for health care (known as *tutelas)*, access appears to remain a problem.

As coverage expanded, individuals' out-of-pocket expenditure in health fell rapidly. Today, out-of-pocket expenditures in Colombia are around 14% of total national health expenditure (equivalent to around 1% of GDP), positioning the country at one of the lowest levels in Latin America and lower than the OECD average, which is around 20% as a share of total national health expenditure.

In broad terms the reforms of 1993 can be considered a success as measured both by the extension of financial protection and health care services. In each case, the poorest Colombians appear to have benefitted the most. The reforms of 1993 were strongly progressive. Affiliation increased most rapidly in the poorest quintiles (from 4.3% in 1993 to 89.3% in 2013) and in rural areas (from 6.6% in 1993 to 92.6% in 2013). Improvements in health coverage are evident, as demonstrated in some key metric such as reductions in unmet health need, reductions in waiting times, increased preventive health care consultations and increased perceptions of quality by service users. As with extension of financial protection, improved access to services has mostly benefited the poorest Colombians: reported unmet health care needs in the past month fell from 33.2% surveyed in 1993 to 2.0% in 2013 (compared to 7.3% and 0.9% respectively amongst the richest quintile) and preventive health care consultations (in the 12 months prior to being surveyed) rose from 30.1% of the population surveyed in 1993 to 62.8% in 2010 (compared to 50.2% and 78.9% respectively amongst the richest quintile).

The share of Colombians reporting that health care services overall are "good" or "very good" has increased from 78.5% of the population in 2003 to 84.6% in 2010, with the steepest increase observed in the poorest quintile. Waiting time for a general consultation has fallen from 6.4 days in 2003 to 3.8 days in 2010, although on this measure the poorest quintiles already had better access to care than wealthier quintiles.

Although Colombia's path towards UHC has frequently been threatened, steady progress and system strengthening have been maintained

Colombia's steady progress toward universal health coverage (UHC) demonstrates sustained political commitment and effective governance, both vital elements given the factors that might have easily derailed the reform programme before now. First, as mentioned, a significant and unexpected economic recession at the end of the 1990s led to a sharp contraction in employment rates and the resources available for health. The government responded by redirecting funds to accelerate enrolment in the SR. Another "external shock" was the Constitutional Court's ruling in 2008 that the benefits package in the CR and SR regimes should be equalised for children aged under 18 years within a year, and a timetable set out for the gradual and sustainable unification of the benefits packages for the rest of the population.

Internal issues have also threatened the system. In particular, key actors in the system were not ready for managed competition. Financial supervision, for example, has been weak, leading to well-publicised cases of misuse of funds by EPS. There was also mismatch between what Law 100 required of municipalities, some of whom have populations of only a few thousand, and what they were reasonably capable of. Local government authorities (ET) were given complex functions on both the supply and demand side: being required to integrate federal, state and municipal revenues, and purchase and administer all health care services for their populations. There have been several well-publicised cases of misuse of funds by municipalities, including political clientelism. Likewise, public hospitals saw direct reimbursements from municipalities reduced as people enrolled in insurance schemes and paid out-of-pocket less often. But public hospitals were not used to selling to services in a competitive market, and had weak administrative and accounting infrastructures to price these services correctly. In seeking to address these issues, subsequent reforms have left the main structural elements created by Law 100 in place, and sought to further improve the governance and delivery of health care in specific areas such as primary care or rural and remote care (described further in Chapter 3).

Colombia has also started to build a sophisticated information infrastructure to monitor health care activities, costs and quality. SISPRO (*Sistema Integral de Información de la Protección Social*) is the data warehouse for services and care provided across the Colombian health system. It brings together several databases that cover financing and health accounts; individuals' health care needs, risk factors and service utilisation; distribution and characteristics of insurers; and, distribution and characteristics of providers, including some indicators of quality and outcomes. Once fully operational, SISPRO will support health system monitoring and planning, as well as providing public access to key health system statistics and reports. Its website (www.sispro.gov.co) already allows users to construct search queries on insurance coverage, service use and high-level outcomes such as mortality. More detailed information on service quality and outcomes is lacking, however.

Colombia has also become a regional leader in key activities. Its health technology assessment agency, IETS, is one of the most advanced in Latin America, for example. Similarly, trade bodies recognise the Colombian Patent Office as being fast and technically competent in its assessments. Other examples include Colombia's regional leadership of *Plan Andino* (to reduce teenage pregnancy rates), prevention and control of chikungunya (a vector-borne disease), intersectoral approaches to better nutrition and food security. External assistance from development agencies has evolved from being nation-wide system building to technical assistance on specific policy needs, such as addressing waiting times. The nature of assistance has also changed from being directive input to coaching and knowledge brokering, signalling a maturing of Colombia's institutional and technical capacity.

Access and quality in Colombia's health care system

Colombia has achieved generally improved access to health care services, although important regional differences persist. In common with most health systems, Colombia is trying to strengthen primary care and pivot the health system away from avoidable use of hospital beds. Colombia's first priority must be to collect and publish more information on health care quality and outcomes. In particular, more information on the quality of primary care is urgently needed to benchmark local services and drive continuous improvement. Transparent reporting of quality and outcomes will enhance the status of the sector and assist in developing a specialist primary care workforce, a closely linked priority. Continued innovation in the models of care, especially in rural and remote areas, is also needed.

Primary care services are intended to be the focal point in meeting population health needs and co-ordinating care

Colombia's primary care system (*Atención Primaria en Salud*, APS) is seen as fundamental to meeting population health care needs. A governance framework to support the role of primary care within the wider health system was brought in by Law 1438 of 2011, specifying co-ordinated action between government, health care insurers and providers, as well as society, to place APS front and centre of efforts to improve population health. The ministry has set out an expectation that 90% of complaints should be resolved at primary care level, without the need for referral to secondary care. There is a clear hierarchy of service levels, with the primary level serving as the main point of entry into the health system for patients, with the exception of emergency services. A registration system is in place, and referral from a primary care provider is necessary to access subsequent levels of care. Primary care providers increasingly work within multidisciplinary teams.

In addition, reforms in 2012 sought to improve prevention and early detection of certain conditions such as cervical and breast cancer, or problems in childhood development, through a programme known as *Protección Específica y Detección Temprana* (PEDT). Clinical guidelines were produced to support these initiatives, and EPS and IPS are required to report activities related to the PEDT priorities. Integrated care networks focused on long-term conditions are an increasingly important feature of Colombian primary care. The *Politico de Atención Integral en Salud* (PAIS, or integrated health care policy) is a new model of care that aims to better integrate primary care, public health activities and wider intersectoral action at community level. Enhanced work force capacity and new technologies are also addressed within the PAIS programme. Individual and population risk management is a central element, and is expected to deliver the ambitions of the *Plan Decanal de Salud Pública*, or Ten-Year Public Health Plan. PAIS remains, however, a set of policy plans that remain under discussion and has yet to deliver real service reconfiguration on the ground.

The APS workforce in Colombia, in general, lacks specialist training. After graduating from medical school, Colombian doctors may spend their careers practicing in primary care (or in hospital emergency departments) without any further training. In some cases, employers (whether IPS or EPS) may organise training on specific topics, according to local health needs, but this is neither systematised nor particularly incentivised. These loose arrangements persist despite the fact that a recognised speciality of family medicine has existed since the 1980s, comprising three years' postgraduate training. Seven medical schools (the majority in Bogotá) offer this programme, but less than 500 doctors have taken it up over the past three decades. A number of reasons for the low popularity of specialist training have been suggested. First, doctors in Colombia must pay out-of-pocket for any postgraduate training they undertake. Second, specialist training is not compulsory to practice as a primary care doctor. Third, salaries and working conditions in APS services are of poor quality (with contracts of only a few months' duration, for example), limiting the incentives to pursue this career path.

Colombia's Ministry of Health recognises that modern primary care requires a workforce with specialist training, continuing professional development, and attractive working conditions. It intends to create 5 000 family medicine specialists over the coming years. Law 1164 in 2007 defined core professional competencies for APS (as well as other clinical specialities) that have been embedded in the PAIS model of primary care delivery, described above. Linked to this, the ministry has taken further steps to specify a training curriculum, at both undergraduate and postgraduate level, to reinvigorate the speciality of family medicine. The curriculum places strong emphasis on preventive, continuous and person-centred health care. Thirty medical schools across Colombia now offer a one-year postgraduate course in family medicine.

Primary care services in rural and remote areas remain unequal but have received targeted investment

Despite efforts to embed effective primary care across the country, unequal resourcing remains a problem. The density of generalist (primary care) doctors, varied from less than 2.5 per thousand population in the departments of Chocó, Guanía, Vaupés and Vichada to over 17.0 in the departments of Bogotá/Cundinamarca, Risaralda, Santander and Valle del Cauca (2013 data). In Colombia's 2011 quality of life survey, 16% of the rural population reported foregoing health care needs because of the distance to services, compared to 2.3% of the urban population (DANE, 2011).

There is an expanding range of options to improve access to primary care that use new information technology and communication platforms (ITC). The MSPS and the Ministry of Information Technologies and Communications have a joint programme of work to improve the connectivity of the health sector called *Vive Digital*. Health providers are expected to adopt the use of digital medical records and rely further on telemedicine. According to 2014 data (*Encuesta de Línea Base de Telemedicina*), the vast majority of IPS have adopted the tele-consultation, although little more is known about the frequency and nature of its use.

In terms of new service models, both Law 1438 and the developing PAIS model acknowledge the need for a differentiated model of care in remote regions. In particular, it is recognised that rural and remote areas require a supply-led model of health care, rather than the demand-led model of managed competition that was prioritised by the 1993 reforms. On the ground, however, it appears that relatively little innovation has occurred in this direction, other than modest efforts to translate information into local dialects or use telemedicine as described above. One exception is the recently approved pilot for community-led health care delivery in the Guainía region, with the support of the Inter-American Development Bank. Guainía is a remote province where over 85% of the population is indigenous. A single insurer/single provider delivery model has been developed, based upon a public-private partnership with both demand- and supply- side subsidies, including pay-for-performance. Close involvement of local indigenous communities in the objectives and design of the model was a prominent part of the initiative. In addition, the MSPS's *Programa de Atención Psicosocial a Víctimas de la Violencia* has primarily benefitted rural populations.

Quality and value-for-money in primary care and the health system more widely remain largely unknown

Despite ambitions that APS be front and centre of the health system, not enough is known about the activities, costs and outcomes of primary care in Colombia. Some key metrics, such as increasing numbers of preventive health care consultations and reductions in infant mortality, demonstrate the important contribution that APS services make in meeting Colombia's health care needs. Beyond these high-level measures, though, a more detailed picture of the performance of the APS sector is lacking. A significant volume of data around APS services is routinely collected, but most of it pertains to inputs, activities and costs – little relates to quality or outcomes.

SISPRO currently contains high-level outcome measures such as mortality. More detailed information on service quality and outcomes is lacking, however. This is a crucial impediment for users to make informed choices of insurer and provider based on the standard of services, as envisaged when the health reforms of the early 1990s were introduced. Moreover, although SISPRO has evolved into a relatively user-friendly platform, there seems to be little knowledge among the general public on the availability of that information and how such information could be used to compare providers and payers. In specific areas, such as cancer care, there is a strong need for the collection of more detailed data on basic aspects of process and outcomes like survival rates, which are virtually inexistent even in the leading national institutions.

Colombia has begun to develop a number of public health observatories and national surveys. These are not, however, true patient or disease registers that could be used for continuous quality monitoring and improvement. The *National Cancer Observatory*, to give one example, publishes mortality rates but these data are drawn from national surveys, not from providers. They give some indication of the combined impact of clinical services, public health and other interventions at municipal, departmental and national level, but are of limited use in directly understanding providers' quality of care. The situation in primary care is of an even greater lack of data on performance and value.

In broad terms, there are no national systems in place to deliver feedback to individual providers about their performance, or how their performance compares with local and national peers. Some EPS are developing mechanisms to provide their IPS network with this type of information. But aside from an incipient benchmarking and incentive system for the prevention and management of chronic renal failure, a national approach to directly monitoring providers' quality of care is lacking.

A richer information system should underpin incentives to improve provider quality, eventually including innovations in payment mechanisms

A richer information system, with a focus on the outcomes achieved by primary care and providers more widely, should be Colombia's first priority. Development of more effective monitoring of quality and outcomes is a priority because IPS currently has very few incentives to improve performance. Given Colombia's epidemiologic transition, the focus, initially, should be on quality and outcomes for key chronic conditions such as obesity, diabetes and cardiovascular disease, as well as mental health. Validated metrics of the quality of primary care for these conditions are well established internationally (such as rates of avoidable hospitalisation), and should be adopted by Colombia. Colombia submitted some data on avoidable hospitalisations to the OECD's *Health Care Quality Indicators* project for the first time this year, but more work is needed to improve the data's quality and comparability before they can be benchmarked next to OECD health systems.

The model being developed within PEDT, where EPS and IPS are required to report activities related to prevention and early detection activities, provides a nucleus for something that could develop into a sophisticated monitoring system – if the focus shifts to collecting outcomes as well as activities. Colombia's SISPRO databases are strong platforms from which to build further. The emphasis must now be on defining, collecting and analysing more quality and outcome measures. Most other OECD health systems are rapidly developing in this area. Health systems in the Nordic countries, the Netherlands and Israel, for example, provide good examples of how richer outcomes data has led to service improvements.

Colombia should move to ensure that it has complete coverage of the relevant denominator populations, by developing a fuller set of patient or disease registers (for example, by registering all diabetics in Colombia). Colombia should make full use of the advantage it has in the SISPRO initiative, by ensuring that all patient registers have compatible formats from the outset. Other countries with long histories of patient registers (often developed spontaneously by pioneering clinicians), now find themselves struggling to achieve compatibility across them. Colombia can leap-frog this obstacle by developing a modular approach, within a common SISPRO framework.

An active programme of audit and research should be also encouraged, with a focus on transparent comparison of providers' results. Comparing the performance of Colombian IPS against international peers (through the OECD *Health Care Quality Indicators* programme) will be an important signal of the system's maturity. Variation within Colombia across EPS and IPS should be also studied closely, both as a means to improve performance overall as well as tackle inequalities. Results on providers' comparative performance should be readily available to EPS and IPS, since this kind of feedback is currently lacking in Colombia. Colombia may wish to restrict benchmarking results to professional groups initially but, as confidence in the validity of metrics grows, findings should be made available to the public.

Once confidence in the validity and comparability of performance metrics is established, Colombia should explore the utility of linking performance indicators to payments. Currently, these services are mainly paid for through fee-for-service (FFS) and capitation, which may limit the incentives towards achieving better outcomes. MSPS has recently commissioned work to explore the feasibility of including P4P in how Colombia pays for APS services, and work on incentivising some aspects of the detection and management of chronic renal failure has started. Continued discussions and piloting of innovations should be encouraged, at both local and national level. OECD primary care systems demonstrate a wealth of models that Colombia could consider, with Portugal and England being particularly sophisticated examples (OECD, 2015; OECD, forthcoming).

A specialist primary care workforce should be developed, focused on tackling chronic non-communicable conditions

A distinct and specialist primary care workforce will be essential to realising Colombia's ambitions of placing APS at the centre of efforts to prevent and manage chronic diseases. In addition to a richer information infrastructure, an important initial step in this direction would be to develop standards and guidelines specific to APS services. Publication of standards and guidelines can also serve to professionalise a sector and enhance its standing – particularly important in health systems which are traditionally hospital-centric. Standards and guidelines also provide the evidence that allows accreditation criteria and quality indicators to be defined. Finally, standards and guidelines will support primary care providers to achieve better quality and outcomes, and can be expected to reduce variation.

Standards and guidelines can then be used as one of the inputs to develop a curriculum for specialist training in primary care. Colombia has already taken decisive steps in this direction, with Law 1164 of 2007 (which set out a new framework for planning, training and regulating health care workers) and other initiatives. It will be essential to ensure that new qualifications, linked to the new training programmes, are validated and recognised by EPS and IPS across Colombia, and that work is undertaken so that clinical and managerial colleagues, as well as patients, understand the enhanced skills and roles that the new qualifications bring.

Development and use of the wider primary care workforce, including nurses and pharmacists, should also be addressed. In Colombia, it is reported that nurses have had their sphere of practice *reduced* in recent years, increasingly spending their time on administrative tasks rather than clinical care. This trend should be reversed. Colombia should work with professional and patient groups, look to international experiences and explore ways in which the wider primary care workforce can contribute to the country's health care challenges. Legal obstacles to extending nurses' and other professionals' roles should be removed, for example by developing protocols which authorise nurses to prescribe a limited set of medications under specific circumstances.

Specialist training, enhanced qualifications and accreditation for excellence should be expected to lead to better contracts and reimbursement. There are plans to improve remuneration and working conditions, and offer scholarships to offset the costs of specialist training. Actual implementation of these plans, however, appears to be at an early stage. It will be important to ensure that actions geared both to the short (for example, more stable employment contracts) and longer term (for example, training scholarships) are taken to make primary care a sought-after speciality. Financial incentives linked to quality and outcomes (i.e. pay-for-performance) are one way in which working conditions can be made more attractive at the same time as improving the performance and professional standing of primary care.

Innovations in service models should be encouraged, particularly in rural and remote areas

Colombia should encourage continued innovation in the delivery models for APS services. The aim must be to provide continuous, person-centred health care, capable of resolving the majority of health care needs. This will require multidisciplinary working, with teams made up of specialist APS doctors, nurses, pharmacists and wider professionals, working to clear standards and guidelines, and within ambitious accreditation and performance monitoring frameworks.

A priority is to address how APS articulate with other parts of the health care system, and to develop integrated packages and pathways of care for individuals with chronic conditions. In Colombia, however, this appears to be inconsistent. The fact that public health services are organised on a territorial basis, whereas clinical services are organised according to SR and CR affiliation, creates obstacles for an adequate integration of provision and continuity of care. There are broad system decrees that all providers of individual and population health care services, as well as EPS, unions, academics etc. should work together, but there are few regulations or incentives on the ground to make this happen consistently. Communications between primary and secondary care when a patient is discharged from hospital, for example, are inadequate, delayed or both. Although PAIS, the new service model for APS, is intended to address this sort of issue, the initiative has yet to deliver real service reconfiguration on the ground.

Defined pathways of care, linked to appropriate standards and indicators, should be developed, with particular emphasis on safety and quality around the transitions of care (for example, upon discharge from hospital). In addition, an increasing number of standards and metrics around integrated care are emerging, such as unplanned readmission rates. Colombia should consider piloting a select number of these nationally or locally, some of which may be linked to financial incentives. The Ministry of Health should also provide additional support to help EPS, IPS and municipal authorities overcome institutional boundaries and develop more effective operational relationships around health promotion, prevention and early detection. Regionally distributed funds, conditional upon a convincing joint operational plan, or linked to performance targets should be considered. These have worked well in other OECD health systems, such as in Italy, Sweden and Japan.

New models of care need to be accompanied by strong governance and a flexible approach to funding

Laws 1122 and 1438 provide sufficient flexibility to allow local service innovation. New models of service delivery such as that being developed in Guainía, which is characterised by supply-side investment and community-led design, should be encouraged. Innovative professional roles should figure prominently in these new service configurations. Colombia should allow a wider range of activities to be performed by nurses, such as monitoring long-term conditions or prescribing some medications. Likewise, pharmacists in areas of need could be allowed to administer vaccines, or prescribe from a limited formulary. Colombia already has a telemedicine strategy in place, and this should be extended to cover more medical conditions and geographical areas. Outreach specialists should be encouraged to act as mentors to local health care workers, building knowledge and confidence, encouraging continuity of care and, most importantly, forging a sustained service network between rural and urban health care providers.

These and other new service configurations will need support from appropriate governance and financing mechanisms. Governance can be particularly difficult in remote areas – because of exceptional health care needs, a lack of institutional capacity, or poor applicability of levers relied upon elsewhere, such as consumer choice to drive better performance. Nevertheless, quality-focussed governance should be at least as prominent in rural and remote services as elsewhere. More demanding performance frameworks for rural and remote health care services are needed, focussed on population health outcomes. This would involve setting targets based on a mix of local and national priorities, and then monitoring, feeding-back and publishing performance against these. In particular, focussed programmes for forcibly displaced people and other victims of the internal conflict, as well as mental health programmes, should be prioritised in rural and remote areas.

Financing, too, should be tailored to rural and remote needs. In broad terms, Colombia intends to shift to demand-led financing where possible across the health system. This is certainly appropriate where patients are in a position to make an informed choice of EPS/IPS. In rural areas, however, low volumes of patients are likely to make this model of funding infeasible. Instead, capitation- and facility-based funding will be needed. Colombia is implementing this, but more ways need to be found to link this type of funding to outcomes. An element of the performance framework for rural and remote health care services could be to make part of a block grant (or additional funds) conditional upon achieving agreed local or national targets for population health outcomes.

Finally, performance of rural and remote health care services can be strengthened by developing its academic base in Colombia. Innovations such as that in Guainía should be studied by independent bodies, emerging lessons disseminated, and elements of the model replicated elsewhere as appropriate. Colombia should consider developing research and teaching institutes of rural and remote health care, such as exist in Norway and Australia. These offer post-graduate diplomas in this specialised field of health care, as well as lead research in the area.

Efficiency and sustainability in Colombia's health care system

Despite recent achievements, the Colombian health sector faces important challenges to maintain and improve efficiency and sustainability. Some of these challenges are common to countries at similar stages of economic development as Colombia, including a rapidly ageing population and declining workforce. Other challenges arise from the specific manner in which the country's health system and its institutions were reorganised after 1993 and the subsequent adjustments made. The envisaged model of managed competition between payers, for example, has not materialised convincingly in practice, creating weak incentives for care quality enhancing activities at the provider level.

Financial sustainability is a particular concern that will need concerted action if Colombia is to maintain its ambition of universal, high-quality health care. Under current arrangements, control around the prices paid for services and around the volumes of services delivered are weak, a strategic approach to capital planning is lacking and fee-for-service payments dominate. There are a number of steps that Colombia could take to strengthen health system performance and sustainability. Key amongst them will be to ensure that EPS evolve into effective and efficient purchasers of care, understanding population health care needs, engaging in prevention and early detection, and awarding contracts to providers based on robust measures of quality and outcomes.

The health system has received substantial funding increases in recent years but continues to run a deficit

Overall, current levels of health funding are aligned with those of most OECD economies. Colombia spent 6.7% of its GDP in the health sector, on average between 2009 and 2013, with over 80% of that spending comes from public sources. Nevertheless, financial strains are apparent. Twenty-one EPS have closed (nine serving the CR, eleven serving the SR and one serving both the CR and the SR) in recent years, for example. It may be that some of these EPS (rightly) exited the market due to inefficiency or poor performance. But the fact that the EPS within the CR as a group reported net financial losses in 2013 and 2014 suggests that there may be a more general systemic problem (PROESA, 2015). These financial losses for EPS within the CR would be even larger excluding funds yet to be received for services obtained via *tutelas*, which are paid retrospectively by FOSYGA (although are often not reimbursed in full).

The situation is somewhat less acute for the EPS within the SR, which reported small net financial gains in 2014. These gains have been dwindling in recent years, however, due largely to increases in expenditures equal to 23% in 2013-14. This rise in spending is likely to reflect expansion in the number of people covered by the SR, as well as equalisation of the benefit package across the SR and CR, and a consequent rise in service use within the SR (medical consultations and diagnostic tests have shown particularly rapid growth). Despite a significant increase since 2011 in the per capita allocation for enrollees within the SR, this does not seem to have been sufficient to counterbalance the substantial and continued growth in expenditures per enrollee.

Financial strain is also apparent from the perspective of providers. In the public sector – where there is more information available – the operational deficit of hospitals reached about USD 62 million in 2012. An assessment of the financial conditions of 955 public hospitals concluded that 45% of public hospitals were at high risk of financial breakdown in 2014 – compared to 32% in 2012 and 42% in 2013 – and a further 14% were at moderate risk (Superintendencia de Salud, 2013). In many cases hospital closures have been avoided by financial rescue operations by the national and local governments.

The generally poor financial health of public hospitals has been attributed to two main reasons. Delays by the EPS in the payment of services provided and complete default on payments owed by those EPS that have ceased operations is one important explanation. A second reason relates to poor operational efficiency and financial management of resources by hospitals, in a scenario of expanding insurance coverage and higher demand for services. This is compounded by a reduction in direct out-of-pocket payments made by a shrinking uninsured population.

Labour market informality presents a significant challenge to raising health system revenues

A key challenge in raising revenues for the health sector is the general issue of informality in the economy. Around half of the total health system funding comes from contributory sources (that is, employer and employee payroll contributions). It has proven difficult to substantially increase this component of funding due to size of the informal labour market, at around 60% of the workforce. High rates of informality narrow the contributory and tax bases and pose obvious financing hurdles to all public sectors. These problems are exacerbated in the health sector, however, because of the Constitutional Court's requirement to expand in the range of services included in the subsidised regime and make them equal to the contributory regime.

One way that the Colombian Government is tackling the informality issue is by moving away from contributory sources of health sector funding. In 2013, employer contributions were replaced by a new tax over net annual profits (*Contribución Empresarial para la Equidad*, CREE) of 9% on corporate income. The CREE is planned to increase to 18% during the period 2015-18, replacing a wealth tax on companies. Even though the introduction of CREE has contributed to a rise in income taxes as share of GDP (to 6.8% in 2013 from 5.5% in the previous year), its effects on health sector budgets are unclear, as CREE revenues are directed to the "social sector" as a whole, not just health.

The judicialisation of health care is also an important threat to sustainability

Any Colombian, at any time or place, may petition for constitutional rights that they believe are denied to them (because of the actions or omissions of public authorities, and where no other means of claiming those rights is available) through a *tutela.* The courts must deliver a decision on the petition within ten days, and the outcome of the *tutela* overrides all other decisions. Individuals are increasingly using this mechanism to meet demands for health care which, if approved, requires their EPS to provide the health care demanded and be later reimbursed by central funds. The growth in *tutelas* is likely to have contributed to the weak financial position of many EPS, as reimbursement by FOSYGA has often been only partial for services not included in the basic package. In the CR, spending on these services represents around a quarter of the total and, remarkably, grew by a factor of 120 between 2002 and 2010. Deleterious consequences arise also for national and sub-national governments, since the funds to reimburse *tutelas* must be met by FOSYGA (in the CR) or local departments (in the SR), and come from sources other than the contributions and taxes introduced specifically to finance health care.

A strong incentive to pursue *tutelas* lies in the pharmaceutical area. The reimbursement of *tutelas*, relating to treatments excluded from POS grew explosively – by a factor of 19 000 – between 2001 and 2008. This alarming situation was worsened by a lack of regulation around the price of medicines excluded from POS until very recently, in contrast to regulated prices for pharmaceuticals included in POS. The national government has taken steps to regain control over such expenditures, mainly by imposing ceilings on the reimbursement of the most common drugs requested through *tutelas* in 2011, but also by including some of these drugs in POS with maximum reimbursement prices.

Deficiencies in the provision of timely and quality services included in the POS also spur legal challenges, particularly among better informed populations. Between November 2011 and November 2012, 75% *tutelas* referred to delays in the provision of services, the majority of which related to services included in the basic benefit package.

System inefficiencies add to the challenges around sustainability

It is certain, of course, that sustainability issues will not be resolved solely by increased funding. There are also systemic inefficiencies in Colombia's health system that need to be addressed to put the system on a sound financial footing. Deficiencies in the information infrastructure, whether as a means to guide user choice or to improve planning, have already been discussed. Another critical issue is that EPS are not fulfilling their potential as strategic purchasers of health care services, as well as poor capital planning arrangements.

Inefficiencies in resource allocation can only be mitigated if accurate and timely information on aspects such as use of services and provision costs are available to guide MSPS and other actors' planning activities. The system of cost data for public providers needs to be improved. Similarly, more user-friendly information needs to be made available for patients to inform their choices of care at all levels of complexity. This would include measures to drive quality-based competition for users. A more active role by the MSPS in collecting and publicising information on payer and provider quality indicators to facilitate choice, as well as more enticing financial and non-financial benefits for providers to apply for accreditation and other markers of higher service quality, is needed.

EPS are key institutions that should manage both clinical risk (through effective prevention, early diagnosis and quality-management of health care providers) and financial risk (by managing demand and contracting intelligently with providers and suppliers). Too often, however, they act as mere financial clearing-houses, lacking effective engagement with either consumers or providers. One example of this concerns the fact that increases in service utilisation has happened to a degree far higher than reductions in unit price, which has led commentators to speculate about the effectiveness of EPS in managing demand and negotiating prices. The fact that provisions in Law 1438 were required to prohibit EPS from acquiring capital assets unrelated to the provision of health services also signals the problems that some EPS had created in the system.

Payment mechanisms for health professionals have remained basically untouched in the 1993 reforms. Currently, they provide weak incentives to continuous quality and efficiency gains, since most professionals are paid solely through fixed salaries (with no link to performance assessment). Furthermore, in many instances contracts are temporary.

A more demanding performance and incentive framework should be used to improve EPS and IPS efficiency

The MSPS has an important role in changing the performance management framework applied to EPS. EPS should add far more value to the system than is currently the case. A key area where a change in the role of EPS could bring about important efficiency gains for the system relates to contracting with service providers. The MSPS should enforce stronger regulation to discourage excessive vertical integration between insurer and provider networks and promote selective contracting, to promote competition between providers. Supporting the EPS with clear contracting guidelines (carefully balanced with adequate autonomy to develop innovative purchasing processes) will be vital. For the managed competition model to succeed, it is important that EPS evolve into fully-fledged purchasers of care, awarding contracts to providers competing for patients based on service quality.

The development of payment-for-performance mechanisms for general doctors and other professionals has been an under-used tool to spur care quality gains. Such mechanisms have been adopted sporadically through a few local initiatives. The MSPS should encourage local experimentation with pay-for-performance. In hospitals, the development of prospective reimbursement mechanisms has been hampered by the lack of information on provider performance, leading to weak incentives for quality-driven competition. Measures to strengthen competition based on quality should encourage the emergence of selective contracting and activity-based financing in the private sector. The public sector must follow suit, to encourage the continuous quality gains that will be especially important given the intended equalisation of benefit packages between the SR and CR.

Defining the basic benefits package as a list of exclusions, rather than inclusions, should be considered

Explicit definition of services to be funded with public resources is not incompatible with a system of universal coverage. Several countries that fund their health systems primarily through taxes or social contributions, ranging from long-established OECD health systems like France, Germany and the United Kingdom, to "emerging" economies such as Thailand, Mexico and Costa Rica, have progressed towards ensuring access to necessary care to most of their citizens, while restricting funding to less cost-effective therapies through explicit inclusion or exclusion lists. Colombia currently has an explicit inclusion list (the *Plan Obligatorio de Salud*). Shifting to an exclusion list should help curtail the need for *tutelas* by assuming, as a starting point, that all medically safe interventions are accessible, unless explicitly listed as excluded from the POS.

Explicit exclusion lists for treatments and therapies must be based on technical criteria, similar to those already employed for defining the inclusion list (i.e. safety, acceptability, cost-effectiveness and budget impact). The creation of IETS, a health technology assessment agency, in 2012 will help in this regard. It will be important to ensure that IETS balances the need between making an adequate assessment of new technologies' safety, effectiveness and cost-effectiveness, with ensuring prompt access to promising innovations. The limits imposed by the government on the reimbursement price of drugs have been an important measure as well, but these limits should be revised periodically to adapt to changing market conditions and not discourage innovation.

Ideally, IETS would be responsible for advising on the updating of the basic package through exclusions and inclusions – which should be done periodically by the government to ensure access to the most cost-effective services and deter further growth in *tutelas*. Measures to improve the quality and timeliness of health care will be equally important to reduce the cost of judicial challenges.

Some countries that have made good progress towards universal coverage have allowed a private insurance market to develop as a supplement to the publicly financed package, offering access to treatments outside the publicly-funded benefits basket (or better amenities in the case of publicly funded services, such as individual rooms for hospital stays). Supplementary private insurance could be adopted in Colombia as well, if the availability of extra services was felt to be important to health care consumers. Careful market regulation by the MSPS, regarding aspects such as equity of access, would be needed if a supplementary private insurance market were to be developed.

Non-contributory sources of funding should be increasingly used

The planned increase in resources for the Colombian health sector in future years, crucial to enabling continued coverage expansions and care quality improvements, should come mainly from pooled financing sources. Countries that have made good progress toward UHC have done so invariably through insurance mechanisms relying on mandatory, pooled funds coming from taxation and social contributions. This is the case, among others, in most European countries, Malaysia, South Korea, and more recently in Costa Rica and Thailand.

Colombia has acknowledged the importance of relying on pooled financing to achieve universal coverage since the inception of the health reforms in the 1990s. Given the already high burden of contributory levies on employers and employees (even compared to other Latin American countries), further health revenue growth will be more feasible if based on general taxation sources, whose increased stability compared to contributory funds is also likely to contribute to the system's long term financial sustainability. The Colombian Government should continue shifting towards general taxes as the main basis of health care financing. It should also maintain its commitment to transfer more revenues to the health sector, as signalled by on-going discussion around the introduction of earmarked "sin" taxes, while limiting user co-payments. It will be important to demonstrate that additional resources contribute to improved system performance. As discussed earlier, a richer data infrastructure on system activities, costs and outcomes will be crucial in this regard. At the same time, the different methods of assessing, collecting and reporting that underlie employees' contributions, CREE and the corporate income tax should be harmonised and strengthened. The potential of these measures to improve revenues for the health system is likely to be substantial.

Broader economic policy initiatives are also needed to reduce labour market informality. Colombia has achieved a modest, but steady, reduction in prevalence of informality by 5% over the past four years. The *National Development Plan 2014-2018* includes additional measures to promote the transition from informal to formal employment, such as improving training and skills, and simplifying registration/affiliation procedures for companies and employee. Co-ordinated action between the MSPS and other government areas such as the Labour Ministry has the potential to create a virtuous circle – as informality reductions will tend to raise cross-subsidies from the CR to the SR.

Another alternative for raising additional revenues for the health sector, whose potential would be enhanced by successful initiatives to tame tax evasion and labour informality, is to broaden the range of general taxes used to finance health. The planned tax on soft drinks with high sugar content currently under discussion by the Colombian Government seems a step in the right direction. Many countries in the OECD and elsewhere have resorted to "sin" taxes (on alcohol and cigarette consumption, for example) as a potential source of additional public funds to pay for health care, while promoting healthy behaviours that are likely to reduce future costs. Colombia should explore this path while carefully considering the implications for an overall progressive tax structure, once again highlighting the need for co-ordinated actions between health authorities and other government ministries.

Capital investment should also be better controlled policies

Providers tend to be largely concentrated in densely populated areas, with a notable increase in the number of private providers in those localities in the last ten years. In contrast, populations living in remote and rural provinces have very little choice of provider even for simple outpatient care. Providers in these areas tend to be public and often struggle with issues such as high operational costs and difficulties to attract and maintain health professionals, which is likely to affect the quality of care provided.

The MSPS could do more to incentivise and regulate more efficient capital investment by both the public and private sector. This would involve stronger leadership by the MSPS on infrastructure planning (perhaps including financial and non-financial incentives for private providers to enter areas currently dominated by the public sector) and revised financial incentives to public providers through the introduction of prospective, patient-based reimbursement mechanisms (virtually inexistent nowadays). In addition, increased effort to submit valid and comparable data to the OECD *System of Health Accounts* will allow better resource-tracking within the Colombian health system, and evaluation of investment decisions.

Conclusions

Over the past two decades, Colombia has impressive progress in extending both health insurance and health services to its population. Nearly 97% of the population have health insurance, entitlements have been equalised between the contributory and subsidised regimes and out-of-pocket has fallen to around 15% of total national health spending. Although some geographic and socioeconomic inequalities in health care use remain, access and outcomes are considerably more equal than might be expected given the country's income inequality.

The financial sustainability of the system, however, is a particular concern that will need concerted action if Colombia is to maintain its ambition of universal, high-quality health care. A key policy priority must be to ensure that the health insurers evolve into effective and efficient purchasers of care, understanding population health care needs, engaging in prevention and early detection, and awarding contracts to providers based on robust measures of quality and outcomes. A closely linked priority on the service delivery side is to strengthen primary care, and place it effectively at the front and centre of the health system as a whole.

Underpinning both of these aims, Colombia's health information infrastructure needs continued investment, so that it is capable of delivering timely and accurate information on providers' activities, outcomes and costs. Colombia's full participation in international benchmarking efforts, such as the OECD's *System of Health Accounts* and *Health Care Quality Indicators*, will be vital to improving and sustaining performance of its health system. This will also enable health system reforms in other countries to benefit from the ambition and dynamism the Colombian health system demonstrates.

Policy recommendations for Colombia

Colombia has many of the right structures and incentives in place to deliver a high-performing health system. In order to deliver efficient, high-quality health care for all citizens and tackle the rapidly growing burden of chronic conditions such as diabetes, on-going reforms are needed. Priority areas for action are:

Improve health system efficiency and sustainability by:

- Developing a more demanding and transparent performance framework around health insurance agencies (*Entidades Promotoras de Salud*, EPS), focussed on population health outcomes, quality of care, financial sustainability and administrative capacity.
- Encouraging innovation and higher performance within the EPS market, for example by publishing performance ratings and allowing stronger performing EPS to absorb weaker ones. Encouraging co-operation within the EPS market where this would be beneficial from a system perspective, allowing EPS to negotiate as a block for pharmaceuticals and other supplies for example, would also be beneficial.
- Addressing the exponential growth in *tutelas* by redefining the basic benefits package (*Plan Obligatoria de Salud*, POS) as an exclusion list. Exclusions should be defined through budget impact and cost-effectiveness criteria, assessed through robust and transparent processes. Improving the quality and timeliness of service provision will also reduce the need for *tutelas.*
- When the POS is redefined as an exclusion list, ensuring that the per capita allocation to EPS for each enrollee (*Unidad de Pago por Capitación*, UPC) is adjusted to reflect additional budget impacts, and regularly revised. Enhancements to the UPC may be needed to support EPS/IPS dealing with specific population health needs, or engaged in medical research.
- Ensuring that the national health technology assessment agency (*Instituto de Evaluación Tecnológica en Salud*, IETS has adequate funds, workforce, political support and international technical assistance to deliver timely and robust transparent cost-effectiveness assessments. Ensuring transparency and public/patient participation in IETS deliberations will support the credibility of its assessments.
- Drawing upon international experience to modify payment systems (to EPS, IPS and workforce) to increasingly reward quality and outcomes, rather than activity. Piloting of prospective, patient-based reimbursement mechanisms over complete pathways of care, such as the DRG system used in other OECD countries, should begin.
- Developing a more strategic approach to infrastructure planning and use of the private sector to meet health care needs, perhaps through financial and non-financial incentives for private providers to enter areas currently dominated by the public sector.
- Delivering preventive care more effectively. In particular, a more demanding performance framework for local governments (*Entidades Territoriales*, ET) is needed, focussed on preventive care and population health outcomes. Mechanisms that bind EPS and ET together in relationships of mutual accountability for population health outcomes, as well as targeted additional resources to support weaker performing ET, will be needed.

Strengthen quality and accessibility by:

- Developing a more demanding and transparent performance framework around IPS, aligned with the performance framework placed around EPS and focussed on the same issues of population health outcomes, quality of care, financial sustainability and administrative capacity.
- Encouraging innovation and higher performance within the IPS market, for example by encouraging EPS to use quality and outcomes metrics in their contracts with IPS, or allowing higher performing IPS increased financial and operational autonomy.

Policy recommendations for Colombia *(cont.)*

- Ensuring the availability of patient-facing information needs to inform choices of care across all sectors in the health system. In particular, transparent information on the quality of local primary care and community care providers should be prioritised.
- Achieving equalisation of the POS offered by the subsidised and contributory regimes. In particular, on-going monitoring will be needed to ensure that accessibility and quality across the two regimes is equal in practice, not just on paper.
- Improving the assurance and monitoring of the quality of care across the system. In particular, the scarcity of reliable quality data is an issue that must be addressed with urgency by Colombian authorities.
- Encouraging wider uptake of voluntary accreditation for providers and strengthening the incentives for its adoption. At the same time, the regulatory capacity of the *Superintendencia Nacional de Salud* should be strengthened so that swift and effective action can be taken against poor performers.
- Clarifying the responsibilities of ET *vis à vis* national authorities, with respect to the assurance, monitoring and improvement of local IPS performance, and supporting them with additional resources and training to fulfil these roles. Following the example of other OECD countries, ET responsibility might focus on primary care and community care facilities.
- Maintaining Colombia's impressive record on improved financial access to care by protecting pooled, pre-paid health funds, increasingly drawn from general taxes as the main source of health care financing.
- Reducing inefficiencies in resource allocation and the planning capabilities of EPS, IPS and ET through accurate and timely information on local health needs, use of services and costs. In particular, Colombia's system of local and national health accounts needs to be modernised and aligned with international norms.
- Extending Colombia's participation in international benchmarking efforts for health system quality and efficiency. In particular, increased effort is needed to submit valid and comparable data to OECD frameworks such as the *System of Health Accounts* or *Health Care Quality Indicators.*

Strengthen primary care and rural and remote care by:

- Developing a richer information system, with a focus on defining, collecting and analysing quality and outcome measures linked to primary care (*Atención Primaria en Salud*, APS) services, as the first priority to strengthen the sector. Comparing the performance of Colombian APS services against international peers.
- Ensuring complete coverage of relevant denominator populations by developing a fuller set of patient or disease registers, and using these to launch a programme of continuous audit and research, focussed on transparent comparison of providers' results. Once confidence in the validity and comparability of performance metrics is established, Colombia should move to link them to payment for APS services.
- Developing a specialist primary care workforce, focused on tackling the rising tide of chronic conditions such as diabetes. This should be underpinned by a more extensive set of APS-specific standards and guidelines and a specialist training curriculum. Clinical and managerial colleagues, as well as patients, should understand the enhanced skills and roles that these new qualifications bring.
- Exploring ways in which the wider primary care workforce can contribute to the country's health care challenges. Legal obstacles to extending nurses' and other professionals' roles should be removed.
- Encouraging continued innovation in the delivery models for APS services, addressing in particular how APS articulate with other parts of the health care system, and developing integrated packages and pathways of care for individuals with chronic conditions.

Policy recommendations for Colombia *(cont.)*

- Defining pathways of care, linked to appropriate standards and indicators, with particular emphasis on safety and quality around the transitions of care (for example, upon discharge from hospital). Using international experienced to select and pilot a select number of indicators of the integration of care nationally or locally.
- Providing additional support to help EPS, IPS and municipal authorities overcome institutional boundaries and develop more effective operational relationships around health promotion, prevention and early detection.
- In rural and remote areas, encouraging outreach specialists to act as mentors to local health care workers, building knowledge and confidence, encouraging continuity of care and, most importantly, forging a sustained service network between rural and urban health care providers.
- Establishing research and teaching institutes of rural and remote health care, such as exist in Norway and Australia. These would offer post-graduate diplomas in this specialised field of health care, as well as lead research in the area.

References

DANE – National Statistics Authority (2011), "Encuesta de Calidad de Vida", www.dane.gov.co/index.php/esp/estadisticas-sociales/calidad-de-vida-ecv/87-sociales/calidad-de-vida/3281-encuesta-de-calidad-de-vida-2011.

IHME – Institute for Health Metrics and Evaluation (2014), "GDP Profile: Colombia", www.healthdata.org/sites/default/files/files/country_profiles/GBD/ihme_gbd_country_report_colombia.pdf.

Javeriana (2014), "Estimación de la carga de enfermedad para Colombia, 2010", www.javeriana.edu.co/documents/12789/4434885/Carga+de+Enfermedad+Colombia+2010.pdf/e0dbfe7b-40a2-49cb-848e-bd67bf7bc62e.

OECD (forthcoming), *OECD Reviews of Health Care Quality: United Kingdom 2016: Raising Standards,* OECD Publishing, Paris.

OECD (2015), *OECD Reviews of Health Care Quality: Portugal 2015: Raising Standards*, OECD Publishing, Paris, http://dx.doi.org/10.1787/9789264225985-en.

Superintendencia Nacional de Salud (2013), "Categorización del Riesgo de las ESE, Vigencia 2011-2012", Superintendencia Nacional de Salud, Bogotá.

World Bank (2015), GINI index (World Bank estimate), http://data.worldbank.org/indicator/SI.POV.GINI.

Chapter 1

Health and health care in Colombia

This chapter presents the demographic and socio-economic context of the Colombian health care system and assesses the burden of disease that the system must address, including the legacy of the internal armed conflict. It describes the legal framework in which the health care sector operates, and how the system is financed. It also reports how Colombia is developing information systems to keep track of activities, costs and outcomes within the health care system.

Progress toward universal health coverage over the past 20 years has been remarkable, with poorer groups primarily benefitting from increased access to services and increased financial protection. Nevertheless, significant socioeconomic inequity continues to characterise Colombian society, and informal employment is a persistent problem that may threaten health sector revenue over the coming years. The health system is also challenged by a rapidly growing burden of chronic disease. Information systems currently give an inadequate picture, however, of whether Colombia is providing high-quality health care in this area.

The statistical data for Israel are supplied by and under the responsibility of the relevant Israeli authorities. The use of such data by the OECD is without prejudice to the status of the Golan Heights, East Jerusalem and Israeli settlements in the West Bank under the terms of international law.

1.1. Introduction

Colombia has achieved great progress towards universal health coverage – measured by enrolment into a formal health insurance scheme – since major restructuring (to consolidate disparate arrangements into two nation-wide health insurance schemes) was undertaken in 1993. Recent data indicate that about 96% of Colombians are now enrolled in formal health insurance. Progress in formal coverage has been accompanied by remarkable improvements over the last 20 years in access to services by disadvantaged populations, while reducing the share of out-of-pocket payments as a source of health care financing, with positive implications for overall levels of financial protection.

This chapter presents the demographic, geographic, socio-economic and epidemiologic contexts in which the Colombian health care system operates, and describes the policy frameworks upon which the system is based. It also explores the major actors and stakeholders involved in the regulation, governance and delivery of health care services. Sources and distribution of revenue for the Colombian health care system are described. Lastly, this chapter describes how data is collected in order to provide information for the planning and management of health care services.

1.2. Health and health care needs in Colombia

During recent years many population health measures have improved in Colombia, such as infant mortality. Large socio-economic and geographic inequalities in health, however, persist throughout the country. This section describes the demographic and socio-economic context of the Colombian health care system and assesses the burden of disease that the system must address, including the legacy of the internal armed conflict.

Colombia's geography and demographic changes constitute a challenging context for the health system

Colombia, the fourth largest country in Latin America, is an extremely heterogeneous country both geographically and demographically. Most of Colombia's 48.3 million inhabitants live in the mountainous regions in the west of the country or along the Caribbean coast, with fewer in the plains and rainforest to the south and east (Figure 1.1). The majority of Colombians are of Caucasian descent, although Afro-Colombian groups represent 10.3% of the population (nearly 4.3 million individuals) and indigenous groups (located mainly in the Amazon, Andean, Orinoquía and the Caribbean regions) represent 3.4% of the population (1.4 million individuals). The Roma people constitute another, yet smaller, minority (DANE, 2007). Urbanisation is happening rapidly. Between 1985 and 2014, those living in urban areas increased by nearly 13%, to reach 76.3% of the Colombian population, while 23.7% of the population lived in rural areas. It is projected that 85% of the Colombian population will live be urbanised by 2050.

Life expectancy at birth is rising and reached 75.2 years in 2013, compared to an OECD average of 80.5 years (OECD, 2015a). Infant mortality rates have decreased from 40 deaths per 1 000 live births in 1970 to 12.8 in 2013 (OECD average, 3.8 deaths per 1 000 live births). Maternal mortality rates remain unacceptably high, however, at 71.2 for each 100 000 live births – ten times higher than OECD average of around seven deaths per 100 000 live births. Both maternal and infant mortality rates are higher in rural areas and in minority ethnic groups – but they are nevertheless decreasing, largely due to improvements in sanitation.

Mortality rates decreased from 488 deaths per 100 000 inhabitants in 2000 to 390 deaths per 100 000 inhabitants in 2011 (MSPS, 2014a). At the same time, fertility rates have been falling. In 2005, for each 100 women of child-bearing age (15 to 49 years), there were 38 children between 0 and 4 years, in 2013 it had fell to 35, and for 2020, it is projected that it will be around 34. Fertility rates remain higher in rural than in urban areas. In 2012 it was estimated that Colombia's global fertility rate was 2.8 and 2.0 children per woman in rural and urban areas respectively (World Bank, 2015a). As a result, Colombia's shifting population pyramid resembles that of OECD economies, with a narrowing younger base and expanding numbers of older adults (Figure 1.2; DANE, 2008).

Figure 1.1. Map of Colombia: Selected configuration of main regions by department

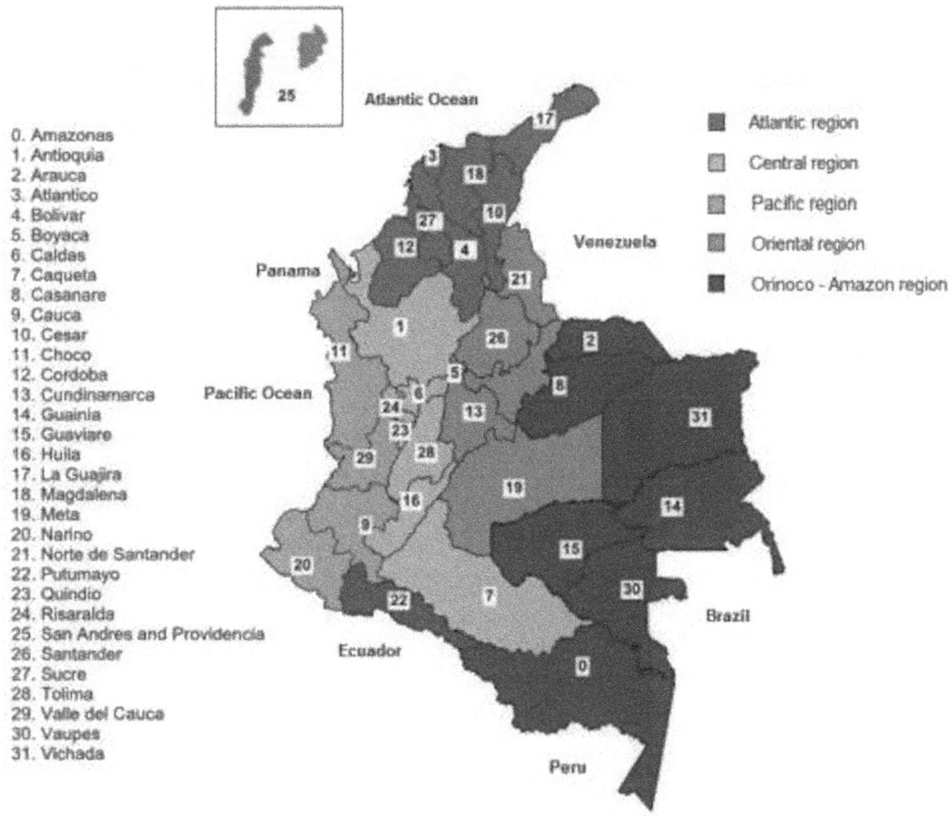

This map is for illustrative purposes and is without prejudice to the status of or sovereignty over any territory covered by this map.

Note: There is no single official grouping of regions. Departments are grouped here based on discussions with the Colombian Ministry of Agriculture and Rural Development (MADR) and DANE information used for various national surveys and analyses.

Source: OECD (2015), *OPECD Review of Agricultural Policies: Colombia 2015*, http://dx.doi.org/10.1787/9789264227644-en.

Figure 1.2. Population pyramid in Colombia by sex and age, 2005, 2014 and projections 2020

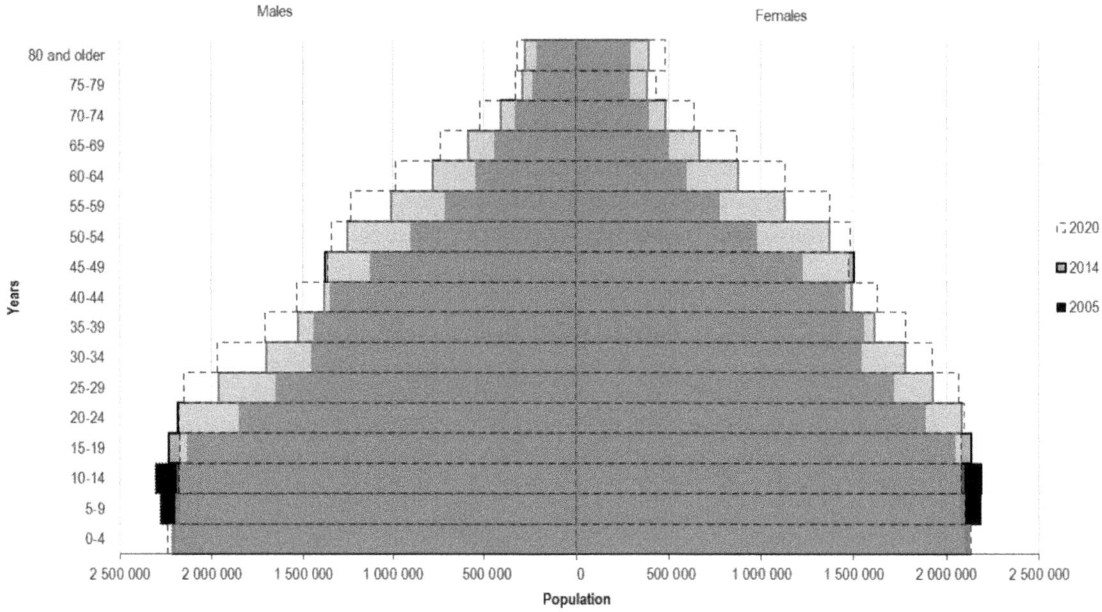

Source: MSPS (2014), *Análisis de situación de salud: Colombia 2014,* www.minsalud.gov.co/sites/rid/Lists/BibliotecaDigital/RIDE/VS/ED/PSP/ASIS_2014_v11.pdf.

Wealth and productivity are improving but large socioeconomic inequalities persist

Colombia has maintained stable economic growth over the last decade. Mainly dependent on commodities export (minerals, coffee and other raw materials), Colombian gross domestic product (GDP) grew 3.9% per year between 2003 and 2008, and 2.7% per year between 2008 and 2013 (OECD, 2015c). Colombian GDP per capita was USD PPP 12 750 in 2013, up from USD PPP 6 611 per capita in 2000 (standardised to 2015 prices in each case). The gap in GDP per capita between Colombia and OECD economies has started to narrow, although remains large (Figure 1.3).

Figure 1.3. GDP per capita in Colombia and OECD countries

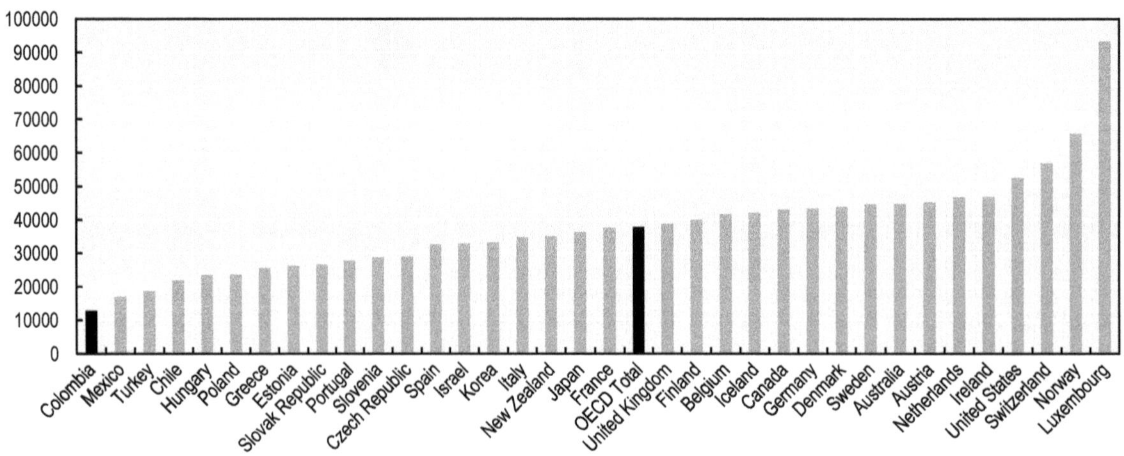

Source: *OECD National Accounts Statistics,* http://dx.doi.org/10.1787/data-00001-en.

Poverty, as measured by the percentage of people living under the national poverty line, fell almost 20% between 2002 and 2013 (from 49.7% to 30.6% of the population; World Bank, 2015b). Even though poverty in the country as a whole is decreasing, large disparities between different regions persist. Colombia, in fact, has one of the highest inequality levels in Latin America and is higher any OECD economy, as measured by P90/P10 income ratio[1] in 2011 (Figure 1.4). Moreover, the income Gini coefficient[2] for Colombia was amongst the world's highest in 2012, reaching 53.5 (compared to an OECD average of 32.2), although this has been decreasing (World Bank, 2015c). Poverty is concentrated in remote departments on the Pacific coast (such as Chocó, Nariño and Córdoba), but also characterises inland departments that were heavily affected by the internal conflict (such as Boyacá, Tolima and Huila).

Figure 1.4. Inequality as P90/P10 ratio in 2012

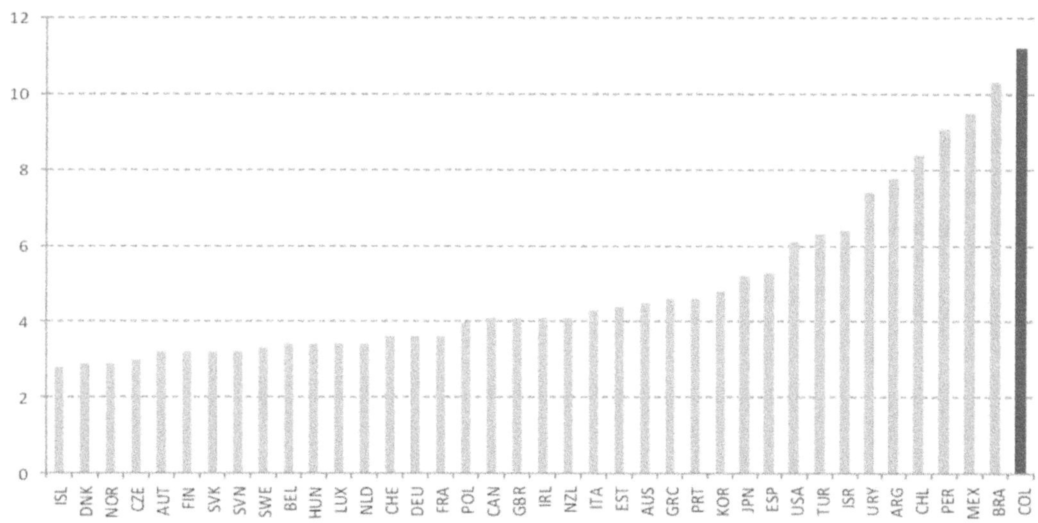

Note: The P90/P10 ratio shows the upper bound income of the ninth decile in the income distribution to the upper bound income of the first decile. 2011 data for OECD economies.

Source: *OECD Income Distribution Database*, http://dx.doi.org/10.1787/data-00654-en and SEDLAC (CEDLAS and The World Bank).

Like most emerging economies, Colombia is characterised by a high incidence of informal employment. Several definitions of informality are in use, such as employees without a written contract, self-employed people without registered activity, or workers not contributing to pensions and/or health insurance. The prevalence of informality in Colombia changes depending on the definition used, although all definitions place the informality rate in a range between 59 and 75% of the workforce in the country as a whole (OECD, forthcoming). These estimates reflect the rate published by the Colombian Statistical Office of 59% (DANE, 2013). These rates of informality are somewhat higher than what would be expected given the country's economic development. Informality tends to be concentrated among low-skilled workers, workers aged over 55 and in traditional sectors with low productivity. Furthermore, informality rates are lower in metropolitan areas (*cabeceras*) than in the rest of the country. Importantly, formal jobs tend to pay nearly three times more, on average, than informal ones and the gap has been widening in recent years due to a steady growth of formal work sector earnings.

Colombia ranks 98 out of 187 countries in the Human Development Index (HDI, a summary measure that combines indices of health, education and living standards;

UNDP, 2014). In 2013, the HDI in Colombia was 0.711 points, improving from 0.708 in 2012. Colombia is at a lower level in comparison to countries such as Chile (0.822) or Mexico (0.756). More than one in three households (37%) report basic unmet needs. This figure is decreasing, but remains higher in rural areas (DANE, 2011a). Adequate housing extends to 90% of the country, for example, but is much lower in poorer departments such as Córdoba (41%) and La Guajira (46%). Water treatment plants (to provide drinking water) are present only in 56% of rural areas, compared to nearly 100% of urban areas.

Colombia's major health care needs now stem from chronic conditions such as cancer and diabetes

Colombia and other countries in the Latin American region are often described as having a "triple burden of disease". Chronic conditions such as cancer, heart disease or diabetes (also known as non-communicable diseases, NCDs) now place the greatest demand on Colombia's health care system, accounting for 71% of all deaths (Figure 1.5). At the same time, deaths due to communicable, maternal, perinatal or nutritional conditions (12%), and deaths due to injuries (17%) remain substantial.

The main cause of death in 2012 was cardiovascular diseases, representing 28% of deaths (although such deaths are becoming less common, having fallen from an adjusted rate of 166 in 2005 to 147 deaths per 100 000 population in 2012; MSPS, 2014a). Cancers were the second most common cause of death, amounting to 17% of all deaths in 2012.

Figure 1.5. Causes of mortality in Colombia in 2012

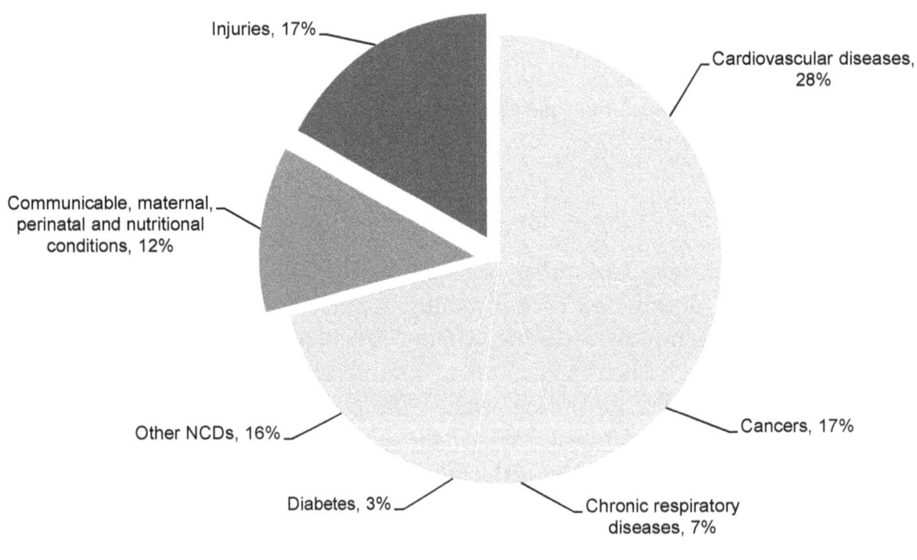

NCDs: Non-communicable diseases.

Source: WHO (2014), "Colombia", www.who.int/nmh/countries/col_en.pdf.

According to a study by the Javeriana University, Colombia's burden of disease (measured by DALYs) was 269 per 1 000 inhabitants in 2010 (Javeriana, 2014). 78% of this burden was attributable to ill-health (measured as years lost to disability, YLD), and the remaining 22% to premature mortality (measured as Years of Life Lost, YLL). Of the total DALY burden, 83% was attributable to NCDs, while 9% and 8% were attributable to communicable diseases and injuries respectively. These figures show a substantial shift from 2005, when there was a larger share of disease burden due to communicable diseases (15%), and a lower share due to NCDs (76%).

The five leading causes of DALYs in this study were hypertensive heart disease, unipolar major depression, violence, dental decay and chronic obstructive lung disease (Figure 1.6, Javeriana, 2014). Depression has risen above diarrhoeal diseases, respiratory infections and birth complications to become the second most substantial burden of ill-health in Colombia (representing 37.8 and 68.8 DALYs for men and women respectively per 1 000 inhabitants in 2012), signalling the importance of developing effective mental illness prevention and treatment programmes in the country. Estimates by the Institute for Health Metrics and Evaluation show somewhat different leading causes of DALYs for Colombia in 2010, where the leading cause of DALYs is interpersonal violence, followed by ischemic heart disease, major depressive disorder, HIV/AIDS, lower back pain and road injuries (IHME, 2014).

Figure 1.6. Biggest causes of burden of disease in 2010

DALYs per 1 000 inhabitants

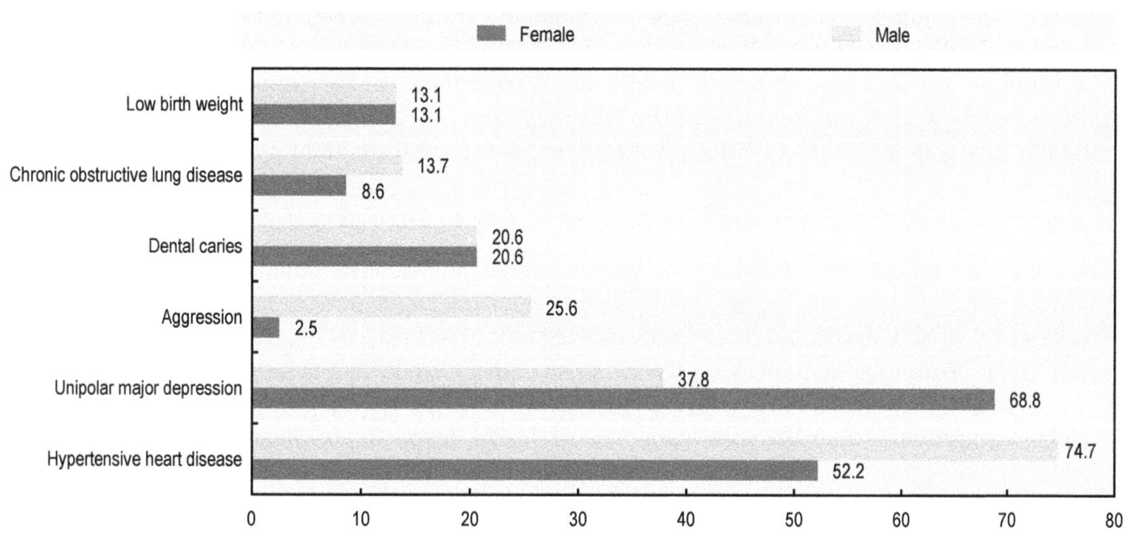

Source: Javeriana (2014), "Estimación de la carga de enfermedad para Colombia, 2010", www.javeriana.edu.co/documents/12789/4434885/Carga+de+Enfermedad+Colombia+2010.pdf/e0dbfe7b-40a2-49cb-848e-bd67bf7bc62e.

Non communicable diseases are closely associated with avoidable risk factors such as obesity, smoking and harmful alcohol consumption. The prevalence of overweight (Body Mass Index >25 kg/m^2) was 35% in Colombian women aged 16-64, compared to 34.1% in men (2010). More Colombian women are obese (Body Mass Index >30 kg/m^2) than the OECD average (20.1% vs. 17.9%) (OECD, 2015a). Colombian men, however, are healthier than average on this measure (11.5% vs. 17.4% OECD average). Overweight and obesity is a growing problem within younger age groups. According to the National Nutritional Survey report (2010), 18.1% of girls aged 5 to 17 years and 16.9% of boys were overweight or obese, approaching the OECD average of 21% and 23% respectively. More promisingly, the prevalence of smokers in Colombia was 17.2% for men and 6.9% for women in 2012, significantly lower than OECD averages of 24.2% and 15.5% respectively. Alcohol consumption in Colombia is relatively low. Colombians (above 15 years of age) consumed 4.4 litres of alcohol per capita in 2012, half of the OECD average of 8.8 litres. Nevertheless, about 11.1% of the Colombian population 12-65 years of age have high-risk or harmful consumption of alcoholic beverages, representing 1.9 million men and 0.6 million women (Observatorio de drogas de Colombia, 2013).

Significant challenges, however, around infectious disease control, maternal and child health and prevention of injuries, persist. BCG-vaccination coverage was around 89% in 2012, but in some regions such as Guaviare, Vaupés, Vichada, Cundinamarca and Cauca coverage fell to less than 70% (MSPS, 2014b). Communicable diseases particularly affect vulnerable population groups including the young, women, rural and indigenous populations. In contrast, injuries (accidents, self-inflicted injuries and violence) most commonly affect males between ages 5 to 44 years (Bernal, 2012). Of some concern, Colombia shows a worsening trend in the incidence of children with birth weight below 2 500 grams, currently at about 9%. It is estimated that 76% of the low birth weight children are grouped in the poorest population.

Despite these challenges, Colombians' perception of their health status has improved. According to a 2007 national health survey, 16% of the population (aged between 6 and 69 years) estimated their health was "very good", 56.2% considered their health was "good", 25.4% considered it "average", and 2.2% "bad" or "very bad" (Rodriguez, 2009). Within the low-income population, health status perceived as "very good" or "good" rose from 58.6% in 1997 to 74.4% in 2010. This may relate to Colombia's rapid expansion of health care insurance amongst disadvantaged groups, as described later in the Chapter.

Regional and socioeconomic inequalities in health care access persist

Despite recent improvements in health insurance coverage, the poorest and most vulnerable socio-economic groups still face greater obstacles to access health care when compared to the wealthier socio-economic groups (as further described in Chapter 2). Although preventive health care consultations (in the 12 months prior to being surveyed), for example, rose from 30.1% in 1997 to 62.8% in 2010 in the poorest quintile, in the richest quintile this number rose from 50.2 to 78.9% respectively, meaning that work to reduce socio-economic inequalities to health care access remains.

Access to health care services in Colombia is more difficult in rural areas. Many rural areas are inhabited by indigenous communities, who may have beliefs, traditions and models of health care that are substantially different to the western health care model that is typically employed. Further disparities between urban and rural areas become evident when considering that department capitals such as Bucaramanga, Cali and Medellin, have health care providers using very advanced technologies, as well as good quality public services such as potable water, whereas other cities and rural areas fall behind with limited – or no such services (Bernal, 2012).

The legacy of Colombia's long-standing internal conflict represents a significant additional burden of health care need

Colombia's internal armed conflict, which has lasted for over 50 years, is inevitably relevant in any discussion of the country's health and health care needs. Confrontations between armed guerrilla groups, such as the *Fuerzas Armadas Revolucionarias de Colombia* (FARC, Revolutionary Armed Forces of Colombia) and the Colombian military forces have led to widespread violence. Homicide rates, at 28 per 100 000 inhabitants (BID, 2010) are very high compared to the OECD average of 4 per 100 000 inhabitants, although have fallen substantially in the past decade. The civil conflict has also led to the forced displacement and possession of land, forced recruitment and kidnapping, loss of family members (killed or disappearances), injuries and sexual violence; all of these leading to physical illness as well as mental health disorders. With 6.4 million people within the displacement registry (in addition to displaced people not registered), Colombia is included as one of the countries with the highest number of internally displaced people in the world (UNHCR, 2011). In addition to the direct health effects, the Colombian armed conflict has worsened access to health care, education, drinking water and transportation, as well as created stigmatisation of the population on both sides of the conflict (ICRC, 2011). With most victims coming from rural areas, the conflict has aggravated geographic and socioeconomic health inequalities.

Addressing the needs of an estimated 7.1 victims of the conflict between 1985 and 2015 represents a significant challenge to governance and public services. A land restitution law was passed in 2011 (Law 1448, 2011), that seeks to rebuild the social fabric and to take effective measures to aid people who have suffered the consequences of the armed conflict. In addition, the Ministerio de Salud y Protección Social (MSPS, Ministry of Health and Social Welfare) has created *Programa de Atención Psicosocial a Víctimas de la Violencia*, which is a EUR 670 million (USD 737 million) initiative that offers individually-tailored psychosocial and medical care to 3.7 million victims of the conflict, structured over four years. Negotiations between the government and FARC, seeking to bring the country to a post-conflict phase, were initiated in October 2012, in Cuba.

1.3. Achievement of universal health care insurance in Colombia

During the last two decades, impressive reforms have allowed Colombia to reach nearly universal health care coverage and a solid financial protection for the provision of health care services. This section describes the legal framework and continued reforms of the Colombian health care system.

A radical redesign of Colombia's health system in 1993 created a contributory and a publicly-subsidised health insurance scheme

Health insurance and health care services in Colombia were historically provided by a fragmented, poorly regulated set of social security institutes and private enterprises, largely benefitting wealthier Colombians. Health coverage only extended to 24% of the population and was highly unequal: while 47% of the richest quintile had health system coverage, only 4.3% in the poorest quintile enjoyed financial protection from excessive health expenditure. This system came with other problems such as a lack of health coverage for family members and exclusion of individuals with pre-existing health conditions. In addition, public hospitals were widely seen as wasteful and inefficient, characterised by excessively generous payment systems and the hiring of more staff than needed (Orozco, 2006).

In 1993, Law 100 brought about far-reaching reforms by creating the *Sistema General de Seguridad Social en Salud* (SGSSS, or General System of Social Security in Health). This was a big-bang reform that transferred responsibility for planning and purchasing health services to new health insurance agencies called *Entidades Promotoras de Salud* (EPS, see Box 1.1). Law 100 created a national health system by making health insurance mandatory for all those who could afford it, creating a single national pool for insurance contributions, splitting the purchaser and provider functions, and encouraging competition by allowing individuals to choose their insurer, and allowing insurers to selectively contract with providers. Responsibility for managing the financing and operation of health services was devolved locally, whilst steering and regulatory functions were retained and strengthened centrally, through the creation of new institutions (see Box 1.1). Crucially, under Law 100 health care became a legally enshrined right of citizens, rather than a service dependent on charitable supply.

It is possible to become affiliated with the SGSSS through three regimes, namely the contributory, the subsidised and the special benefit regime. In the contributory regime (CR), formal employees provide 4% of their income and the employer 8.5% to a fund called the *Fondo de Seguridad y Garantía* (FOSYGA). The subsidised regime (SR), that receives funding from FOSYGA, includes the low income population, classified by SISBEN (the system to identify households entitled to social welfare programmes); but also includes vulnerable populations such as the indigenous population, displaced persons (approximately 10% of the population), the incarcerated population and others. Risk-equalisation and cross-subsidy exists both within and across the CR and SR, supporting efficiency and social solidarity. The Special Benefit Regime, which includes armed forces, teachers, and a state-owned petroleum company, handles a separate system. This represents about 2% of the population, with expenditure four times higher than the national average (Nuñez, 2012). An additional way to become affiliated to the system is by private insurance (voluntary insurance), includes approximately one million members and has not increased significantly in the last five years.

Box 1.1. Key features of the Colombian health system

Most Colombians become affiliated with the SGSSS through either the contributory regime (CR) or the subsidised regime (SR). Individuals obliged to affiliate through the CR are those with employment contracts, people receiving a pension or self-employed individuals earning at least the minimum wage (in practice, relatively few). Colombians' most frequent contact with the health system is via bodies called EPS and IPS. The ***Entidades Promotoras de Salud*** (EPS, health insurance agencies) are responsible for organising and guaranteeing the provision of health services included in the defined benefit-basket for their enrolled populations. They are also expected to manage population health risk. EPS are required to recruit health service providers to guarantee the access for activities of health promotion, disease prevention, and care at all levels including rehabilitation.

Instituciones Prestadoras de Salud (IPS) are health care provider institutions such as hospitals and clinics. There are approximately 46 000 health providers in Colombia, the majority of whom are concentrated in urban areas. Over the years 2009-11, there were approximately 18 million consultations per year, of which 85% were ambulatory, 10% were emergency services and 5% hospitalisations.

Together, the EPS and IPS in both the contributory and subsidised regimes, and other national bodies such as the national health superintendance constitute the *Sistema General de Seguridad Social en Salud* (SGSSS), or Colombia's national health system. As discussed in later paragraphs, a managed competition model exists, whereby individuals enroll with an EPS of their choice and, at times of health care need, access an IPS of their choice within their EPS network. By law, vertical integration between EPS and IPS is limited to 30% of the insurer's total spend.

Box 1.1. Key features of the Colombian health system *(cont.)*

Health system funding comes from a variety of sources. These are mainly employee and employer payroll contributions for the CR; and national and local tax revenues, as well as cross-subsidisation from the CR in the case of SR. FOSYGA (*Fondo de Solidaridad y Garantía*) is the institution in charge of pooling health funds accruing to the CR, whereas funds for the SR are pooled at the national and (mainly) local levels. EPS receive their revenues through a capitated payment (*Unidad de Pago por Capitación*, UPC) per enrollee, with some adjustment for geographic, demographic and – to a lesser extent – epidemiologic factors. In 2008, the Constitutional Court ruled that the benefits package in the CR and SR regimes should be equalised for children aged under 18 years, within a year. At the same time, the Court required a programme and a timetable for the gradual and sustainable unification of the benefits packages for the rest of the population. This ruling was carried out in 2012. Additional funds were found to meet these commitments, and equal per capita allocations were achieved at the beginning of 2015.

The ***Ministerio de Salud y Protección Social*** (MSPS, Ministry of Health and Social Protection) is ultimately responsible for the funding, design and delivery of health care services through the SGSSS. The ministry develops norms, issues regulations and gives technical assistance to improve health care service delivery. In addition, it designs and implements systems to monitor and assure the quality of health care services, such as the accreditation framework that applies to insurers and providers. The ministry is also responsible for developing and operating the data and communications infrastructures underpinning the SGSSS.

Several of these roles are discussed further in Section 1.4. Other key actors in the Colombian health system include:

The ***National Health Superintendence*** monitors health actors, assesses providers based on a mandatory quality assurance system as well as insurers, based on their facilities, capital, number of affiliates, efficiency and coverage. The National Health Superintendence is also in charge of applying sanctions to health actors not following legal frameworks.

The ***National Health Institute*** (NHI) and ***Public Health Observatory*** are responsible for epidemiologic surveillance. The National Health Observatory is part of the NHI and is responsible for the surveillance of information in public health and to provide recommendations on policies.

The ***Instituto de Evaluación Tecnológica en Salud*** (IETS, institute for technical health evaluations) was created in 2012. This public-private institute has developed its own methodology to perform evaluations of evidence-based technologies and produce guidance and protocols over medicines, procedures and treatments. It makes recommendations on which technologies should be covered by the SGSSS.

The ***Instituto Nacional de Vigilancia de Medicamentos y Alimentos*** (INVIMA, national institute for surveillance of medications and foods) was created in 1993 as an independent agency, to oversee quality control of drugs, biological products, food, beverages, cosmetics, medical devices, natural products and other products that may have an impact on individual and collective health

Colombia is very close to achieving universal health care insurance

Health insurance coverage now reaches 96% of the population, a rapid increase from a baseline of 24% at the inception of Law 100 in 1993. These impressive gains are in large part due to new affiliations in the SR. Those drafting Law 100 assumed economic growth similar to the 1990s, equivalent to 5.1% annually, and anticipated around one-third of the population being included in the CR with a similar number in the SR. These assumptions had to be abandoned in 1999, however, when the economy suffered its biggest recession in many decades with a contraction of 4.1%. Rates of unemployment and participation in the informal labour market increased (Banco de la República, 2006). Nevertheless, rather than abandoning the principles underlying Law 100, an explicit progressive decision was taken to accelerate enrolment in the SR in the early 2000s, as shown in Figure 1.7. More recently, the balance of new enrolments has tipped toward the CR. During 2014, there were 830 000 new enrolees to the system, of whom 73% were in the CR.

Figure 1.7. Evolution of affiliation to the health care system, 1993-2014

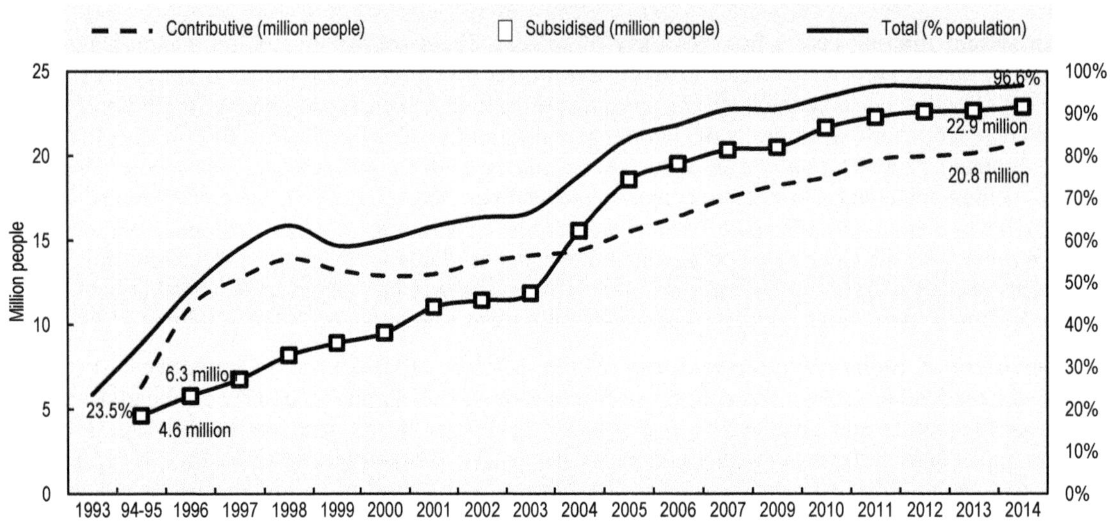

Source: Ministry of Health and Social Protection.

The reforms of 1993 were strongly progressive. Affiliation increased most rapidly in the poorest quintiles (from 4.3% in 1993 to 89.3% in 2013, Figure 1.8) and in rural areas (from 6.6% in 1993 to 92.6% in 2013, Figure 1.9).

Figure 1.8. Growth in affiliation by income quintile, 1993-2013

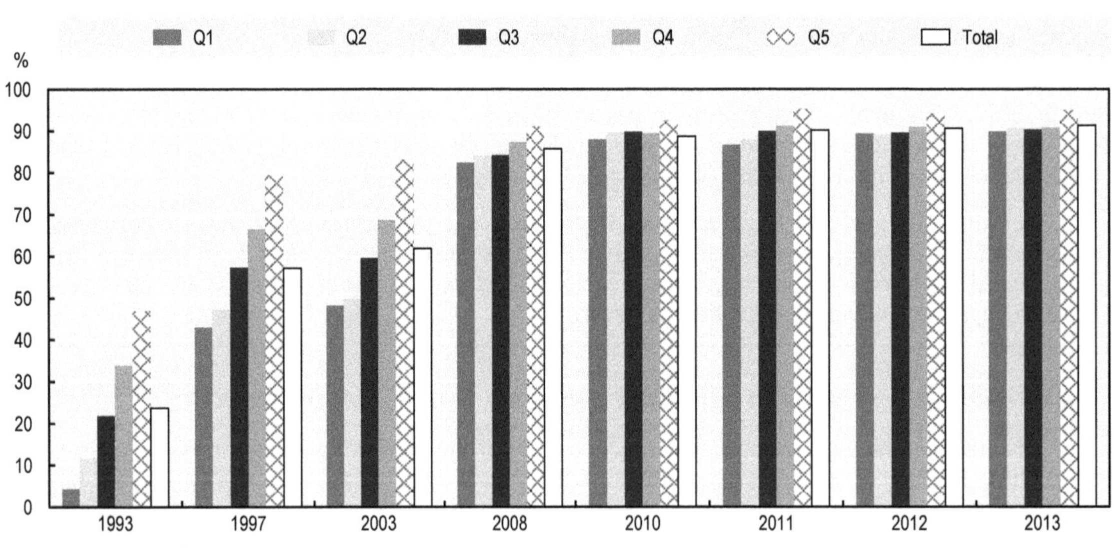

Source: DANE (2011), "Encuesta de Calidad de Vida (Life Quality Survey)", www.dane.gov.co/index.php/esp/estadisticas-sociales/calidad-de-vida-ecv/87-sociales/calidad-de-vida/3281-encuesta-de-calidad-de-vida-2011, with Ministry of Health and Social Protection calculations.

Figure 1.9. Growth in affiliation to the SGSSS, by rurality, 1993-2013

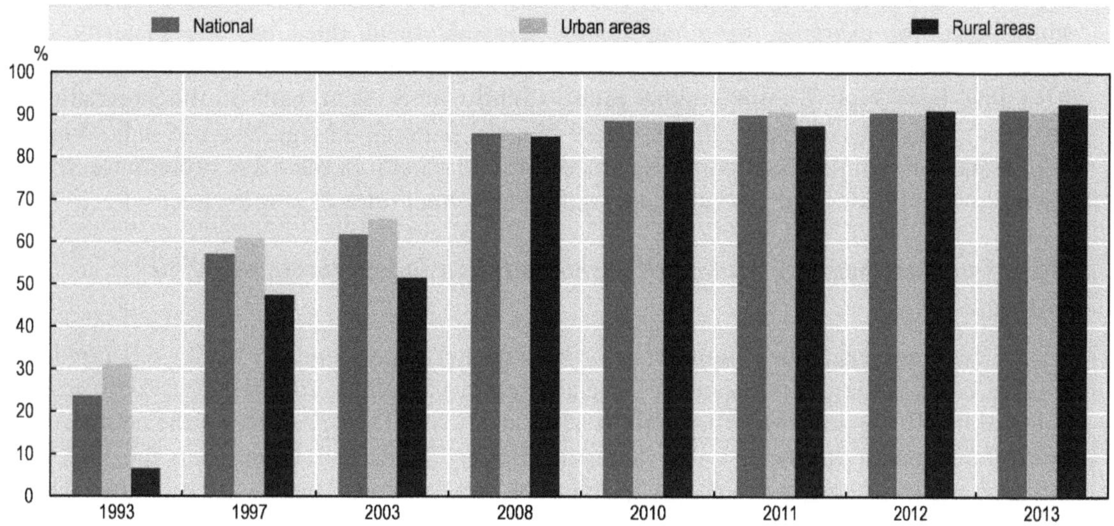

Source: DANE (2011), "Encuesta de Calidad de Vida (Life Quality Survey)", www.dane.gov.co/index.php/esp/estadisticas-sociales/calidad-de-vida-ecv/87-sociales/calidad-de-vida/3281-encuesta-de-calidad-de-vida-2011, with Ministry of Health and Social Protection calculations.

Health system insurance coverage has increased in every region. The difference between them is the type of affiliation; in poorer coastal and Amazonian regions, coverage is largely through the SR, while in wealthier regions such as Antióquia and Bogotá, coverage is mainly through the CR (Figure 1.10). Nationwide, nearly half of the population are affiliated to the SGSSS through the SR, while around 43% are covered through the CR and 2% through the special benefit regime, which leaves around 6% of the population without affiliation.

Figure 1.10. Distribution of health insurance affiliation, by region, 2014

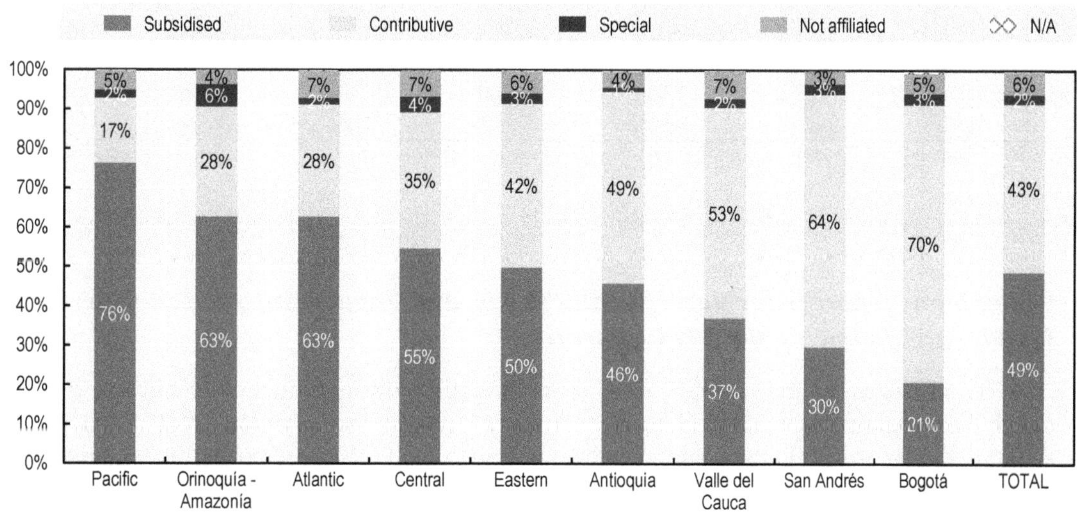

Source: DANE (2011), "Encuesta de Calidad de Vida (Life Quality Survey)", www.dane.gov.co/index.php/esp/estadisticas-sociales/calidad-de-vida-ecv/87-sociales/calidad-de-vida/3281-encuesta-de-calidad-de-vida-2011, with Ministry of Health and Social Protection calculations.

The relationship between unemployment rate and the share of population affiliated to the SR is not always consistent. The departments of Atlántico, Bolívar, Boyacá and Magdalena, for example, have the lowest unemployment rates but the majority of residents nevertheless belong to the SR. Conversely, even though Valle del Cauca and Risaralda have high unemployment rates, slightly more than half of the population belongs to the CR (Guzman, 2014). These unusual patterns emerge because individuals with temporary employment contracts are allowed to remain in the SR. Furthermore, low unemployment rates locally do not necessarily imply high rates of employment.

Out-of-pocket spending on health care has fallen to less than the OECD average

As coverage expanded, individuals' out-of-pocket expenditure in health fell rapidly (Figure 1.11). Today, out-of-pocket expenditures in Colombia are around 15% of total national health expenditure (equivalent to around 1% of GDP), positioning the country at one of the lowest levels in Latin America (Barón, 2014) and lower than the OECD average, which is around 20% as a share of total national health expenditure. The sustained reduction of out-of-pocket expenditure in health is a significant achievement of 1993 reforms.

Figure 1.11. Decrease in out-of-pocket (OOP) expenditure in health, 1994-2013

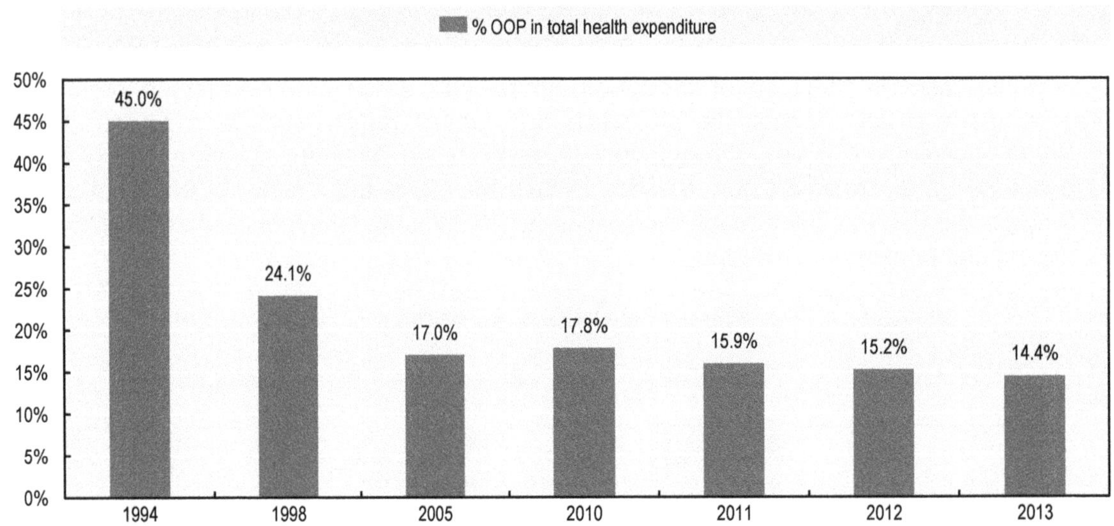

Source: Data provided by Ministry of Health and Social Protection. Health accounts from National Statistics.

Colombians report fewer unmet health needs, and greater satisfaction with health care, following the 1993 reforms

The affiliates to the SGSSS in Colombia, either through the contributory or the subsidised regimes, are entitled to a package of health care services called the *Plan Obligatorio de Salud* (POS, mandatory health plan). The POS is an explicit mechanism of inclusions and exclusions, based on epidemiologic information, cost-effectiveness, preference and safety. The POS in Colombia, defined by the *Comisión de Regulación en Salud* (CRES, Regulatory Commission in Health), currently comprises just under 6 000 activities, procedures and interventions in health and hospital services, and around 750 prescription drugs (MSPS, 2012). Colombia intends to transition toward an explicit exclusion list (Gaviria, 2013). The POS has some general exclusions (such as cosmetic procedures, experimental technology or any other service for which there is no scientific evidence, no known effectiveness or safety) but is, for the time being, primarily defined as an inclusion list. Initially, the POS comprised different packages for the CR and SR, with more generous benefits in the former. Entitlements across the two are now equal.

In broad terms the reforms of 1993 can be considered a success as measured both by the extension of financial protection and extension of health care services. In each case, the poorest Colombians appear to have benefitted the most. Improvements in health coverage as measured by access to services is demonstrated in some key metrics, such as reductions in unmet health care needs, reductions in waiting times for an appointment, and increased perceptions of quality by service users (Figures 1.12, 2.2 and 1.13 respectively). As with extension of financial protection, improved access to services has mostly benefited the poorest Colombians: reported unmet health care needs in the past month fell from 33.2% surveyed in 1993 to 2.0% in 2013 (compared to 7.3% and 0.9% respectively amongst the richest quintile) and preventive health care consultations (in the 12 months prior to being surveyed) rose from 30.1% of the population surveyed in 1993 to 62.8% in 2010 (compared to 50.2% and 78.9% respectively amongst the richest quintile).

Figure 1.12. Proportion of Colombians reporting unmet health care needs in the past month, by income quintile, 1993-2013

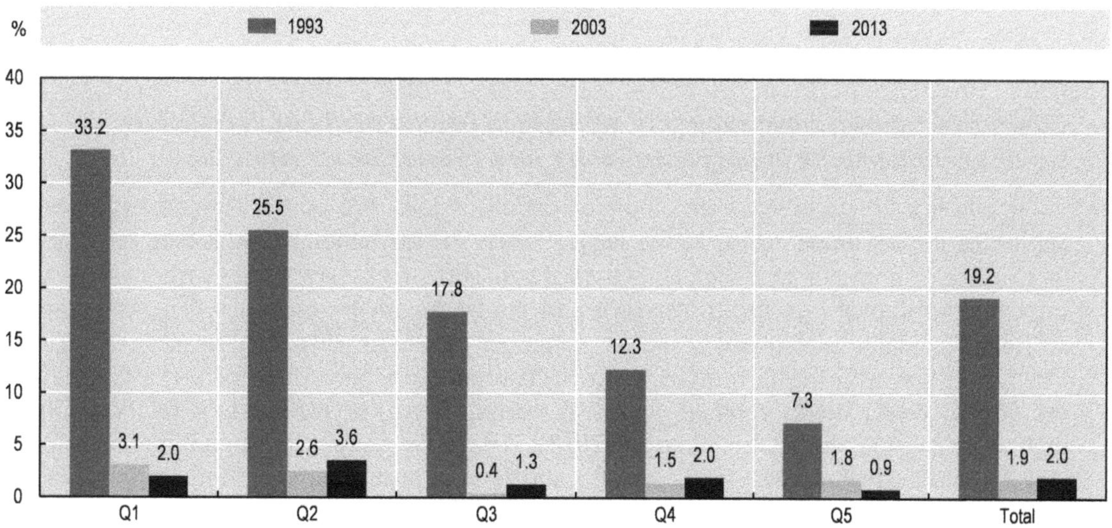

Source: Ministry of Health and Social Protection.

In 2013, there were 4.7 doctor consultations per person in Colombia, somewhat below the OECD average of 6.6 (OECD, 2015a). The vast majority of these health system contacts (85%) were in the ambulatory care sector (MSPS, 2013a). Reassuringly, only 15% of health system contacts involved complex emergency care and/or hospital admissions, which suggests that the system as a whole is not adversely biased toward hospital care.

The share of Colombians reporting that health care services overall are "good" or "very good" has increased from 82% of the population in 2003 to 86% in 2010, with the steepest increase observed in the poorest quintile. Waiting time for a general consultation has fallen from 6.4 days in 2003 to 3.8 days in 2010, although on this measure the poorest quintiles already had better access to care than wealthier quintiles. As discussed in Chapter 2, however, waiting times to see a specialist have almost doubled between 2003 and 2011, from 10.4 days to 19.2 days.

Figure 1.13. Proportion of Colombians reporting that health care services overall are "good" or "very good"

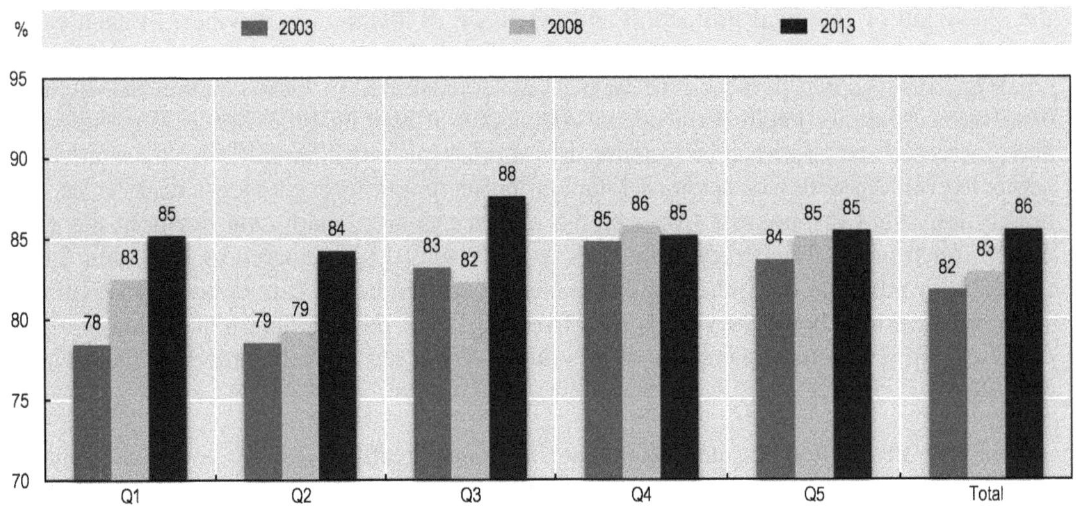

Source: Ministry of Health and Social Protection.

Continued reforms have sought to strengthen primary care and, critically, equalise entitlements in the contributory and subsidised schemes

In the last 20 years since the implementation of Law 100 of 1993, there have been approximately 46 amendments to the legal framework surrounding health care provision in Colombia. A major amendment was made in 2007 with Law 1122, which aimed to improve the delivery of health services and public health programmes. The Law was drafted principally in response to the large number of *tutelas* (discussed in more detail in Chapter 2) that were being brought to the Constitutional Court, both for services within the POS (where patients claimed excessive waiting times) as well as new interventions that were outside the POS (Velasco, 2013). The Law sought to streamline decision making and financial flows between EPS and IPS. It also created a fund for high-cost illnesses, to avoid insurance companies excluding high-cost patients from their services. Chronic kidney disease, several cancers, epilepsy, rheumatoid arthritis and HIV/AIDS were some of the conditions included in the high-cost list.

In December 2010, the Colombian Government decreed a state of emergency for 30 days in order to address problems of financing the health sector. The main objective of the decree was "to avert serious crisis affecting the viability of the SGSSS which imminently threatens continued provision of essential public health services". Based on this declaration the government prepared 11 decrees but the Constitutional Court declared the state of emergency unconstitutional.

Law 1438 of 2011 sought to strengthen health care by embedding primary care as the corner stone of the system, linked to co-ordinated action with hospitals and municipal authorities, to create healthy environments. This law also established a limit of 10% expenditure on administration for the EPS (although did not specify how "administration" should be defined) and placed tighter regulation around the capital investment of EPS. The EPS officially report between 6 and 8% in administration expenditure, while the public audit office has reported that it can be as high as 50% (Contraloría, 2013). The Constitutional Court also banned use of health resources to acquire capital assets unrelated to the provision of health services, in response to some cases misuse of funds by EPS (Corte Constitucional, 2013).

Further reforms to Colombia's health system have been guided by the National Development Plan and National Public Health Plan (Box 1.2). Within this context, a particularly important reform to equalise the entitlements offered in the CR and SR was announced in 2012. Previously, there had been some marked differences in the services covered by each regime. Mammography (breast cancer screening) was covered in the CR, for example, but not in the SR. In July 2012, new regulations established a single POS for affiliates of both regimes (MSPS, 2012) and per-capita funding in the CR and SR is now equal (see below section on how funds are redistributed to EPS through a risk-adjusted capitation formula).

Box 1.2. Colombia's National Development and Ten-Year Public Health Plans

Colombia's ***Plan Nacional de Desarollo 2014-2018*** (National Development Plan, PND) prioritises delivery of high-quality health care services in an equitable manner. The plan establishes four objectives; improving access and quality of health care services; improving population health and decreasing inequalities in health outcomes; regaining trust and legitimacy; and, guaranteeing the financial sustainability of the health care system. Specific actions under each objective include:

Objective 1: Increase access and improve quality of services

To reach this objective, the PND proposes diverse strategies such as innovations in insurance schemes, establishing new rules of affiliation (e.g. immediate for new-borns and enhanced recognition of entitlements to the SR) and the adoption of outcome-oriented contracts to incentivise the competencies within the insurance companies. Also, the PND proposes a programme of public hospital inversion (including State funds and public-private-partnerships) to strengthen physical infrastructure and biomedical, industrial and technological equipment, as well as to improve the management of hospitals.

Objective 2: Improve population health conditions and decrease gaps in health outcomes

The Ten Year Public Health Plan 2012-2021 and the Territorial Health Plans 2012 and 2013 are implemented in harmony with territorial financial plans, emphasising several strategies including:

- Increase in immunisation coverage
- Prevention and treatment of NCDs in order to reduce morbidity and mortality as well as disability due to cancer, cardiovascular diseases, diabetes and pulmonary diseases
- Establishment and monitoring of a strategy on sexual and reproductive rights, where reductions of teenage pregnancy, maternal mortality and any form of sexual violence are prioritised
- Integrated care for the physical and mental health of adults
- Integrated care for the victims of the armed conflict
- Adoption and realisation of the *Politica Integral de Salud Ambiental* (Integral Politic of Environmental Health), oriented on impacting positively on the social and environmental determinants of health

Box 1.2. Colombia's National Development and Ten-Year Public Health Plans *(cont.)*

Objective 3: Regain trust and legitimacy

To reach this objective, the PND has established strategies to strengthen inspection, surveillance and control, strengthen the resource administrative institutions through a centralisation to increase efficiency in the resource stream, simplify processes to provide transparency and reduce transaction costs. Moreover, it is proposed to strengthen the information systems (see below section on SISPRO) and to promote citizen participation.

Objective 4: Guarantee financial sustainability

In order to improve efficiency and support health system sustainability, the PND establishes the following strategies:

- reductions in the costs associated with collection of funds
- revision of risk redistribution mechanisms
- a pharmaceutical policy that strengthens the capacity of the MSPS to control prices
- Stimulate research directed to innovation and development within the health care sector

In addition, Colombia's ***Plan Decenal de Salud Pública, 2012-2021*** (Ten Year Public Health Plan) aims to reduce the inequities in health through an effective right to health for all, improving risk factors and living conditions, and decreasing the existing burden of disease morbidity and disability (MSPS, 2013b).

Further reforms to create a single, national health insurance fund and a unique benefits plan, alongside a new system of service delivery organised by service areas of health care management were announced in 2013. A network of providers was proposed to divide services in three categories; basic, specialised and special; differentiated by the level of complexity of services. However, these reform proposals met with widespread opposition by local authorities that feared this would decrease municipal and departmental autonomy, meaning that they were not passed. In place of a more comprehensive reform, the MSPS has instead issued decrees addressing specific elements of the health system, including strengthening service delivery in remote areas, regulation of biotechnology, updating criteria for affiliation to the SGSSS, and improved financial regulation of EPS (Box 1.3).

Box 1.3. Recent decrees addressing specific elements of the SGSSS

1. Updating criteria for affiliation to the SGSSS

Affiliation criteria are being updated through a new decree which is currently under presidential review and is expected to come into force by end this year. Some major features of the decree are, among others:

- Affiliation will take place once in a lifetime. Disaffiliation will only occur in case of death.
- With a Transactional Affiliation system, unnecessary procedures that used to limit EPS free choice are eliminated. Moving from one EPS to the other will be easier.
- Now, sons/daughters that are between 18 and 25 years old who are economically dependent upon the contributor, may continue as beneficiaries without having to prove they are students.
- New born children will be immediately affiliated to the mother's EPS.

Box 1.3. Recent decrees addressing specific elements of the SGSSS *(cont.)*

2. Improved financial regulation of EPS

Decree 2702 of 2014 established that, since EPS are health risk administrators, they should operate under similar financial solvency conditions as those of insurance companies (minimum capital, solvency margin, technical reserves, investment regime) (MSPS, 2014d). The decree grants EPS that are already operating seven years to adjust to such requirements.

Decrees have also been issued to increase competition around price and supply of new biotechnologies (see Box 1.4) and strengthen service delivery in remote areas (see Box 3.1).

1.4. Key actors in Colombia's health care system

This section describes the roles and functions of each of the major actors in the SGSSS.

Central government holds ultimate responsibility for steering the system, while local government is responsible for public health actions

The *Ministerio de Salud y Protección Social* (MSPS, Ministry of Health and Social Welfare) is responsible for overall stewardship of the health system. The MSPS develops norms, standards and guidelines needed by health insurance agencies and service providers, and gives technical assistance to apply them. The ministry also operates minimum quality standards, as well as the system of accreditation for insurance agencies and service providers. The MSPS also establishes the regime for *Entidades Promotoras de Salud* (EPS, health insurance agencies) and *Instituciones Prestadoras de Salud* (IPS, health service providers) to purchase, supply and extend the provision of health care services. In particular, the MSPS is responsible for regulating the public and private mix of providers, ensuring that access, choice and quality are optimised as far as possible in each locality.

The 1993 reforms largely delegated responsibility for purchasing and providing health care services for local communities to EPS. Very occasionally, however, local governments, or *Entidades Territoriales* (ET), retain this responsibility. This principally applies to the few communities or individuals who remain unaffiliated to the SGSSS. As a result, the number of services directly provided by ET varies greatly. The majority of ET (around three quarters) directly provide between 11 and 40 services; 10% offer between 40 and 100 services; 4% offer between 100 and 200; and 0.4%, corresponding to the five main cities (Bogotá, Cali, Barranquilla, Medellín and Cartagena), offer more than 200 services and 1% (ten municipalities) offer no services because they have no providers (Guzman, 2014). In 504 municipalities (45% of the country's total) health providers are only of public nature. Among these, 73% only have one health provider and 14% only have two.

In addition, *Entidades Territoriales* (which may comprise departments, municipalities, districts, indigenous territories and occasionally regions and provinces) are principally responsible for carrying out public health actions, under the supervision of central government, where a national perspective is relevant. A ministry decree of 2001 identifies ET as the principal bodies responsible for working towards the goals outlined in the Ten-Year Public Health Plans. There is some concern, however, that the mutual and overlapping responsibilities of ET, EPS and IPS with respect to health promotion and prevention of ill-health remains poorly articulated.

Numerous health insurers are responsible for managing clinical and financial risks in their affiliated populations

The *Entidades Promotoras de Salud* (EPS, health insurance agencies) are bodies that individuals, both in and out of formal employment, choose as insurers. At a minimum, their role is to contract with IPS to ensure availability of services listed in the POS, including health promotion, disease prevention, ambulatory and in-patient services, and rehabilitation. Beyond this minimum requirement, however, EPS have a crucial role to play in controlling health system expenditure. They are expected to manage both clinical risk (through effective prevention, early diagnosis and quality management of health care providers) and financial risk (by managing demand and contracting intelligently with providers and suppliers). Few EPS appear to do so effectively, however, as discussed in Chapter 2.

EPS are permitted to provide health services directly, through their own provider network, up to a limit of 30% of their total activity (in monetary terms). This limit was chosen in an attempt to balance the advantages of vertical integration (such as reduced transaction costs, and an incentive to provide less expensive forms of effective care), without losing the benefits of a purchaser-provider split (principally incentives for the provider to optimise the quality and price of their service). The 30% limit was chosen arbitrarily, however, and other OECD health systems pursue the advantages of both fully integrated and fully split purchaser-provider relations. In practice, in Colombia, there is some uncertainty whether the 30% limit on integration is always adhered to. Recent proposals have suggested allowing EPS to fully provide primary care services, with a competitive provider market for secondary and tertiary care.

In 2013, there were 18 EPS in the CR and 35 in the SR (Finol, 2014). One or two EPS accounted for 70% to 100% of the affiliates to the CR in the majority of Colombia's departments, demonstrating concentration of the market. The only market that was not considered as concentrated was Bogotá D.C, were the five principal EPS accounted for 66% of the affiliates. In the SR, one or two EPS accounted for 65% of the affiliates in the majority of departments.

The number of EPS has been falling in recent years. Since 2005, 21 EPS have closed (nine serving the CR, eleven serving the SR and one serving both the CR and the SR). Out of these, 19 were forced to closure by the National Health Superintendence, while two of them closed voluntarily (due to market forces). A decree issued in 2014 sets out more clearly the expectations around the financial performance of EPS. It states that EPS have seven years to reach the minimum amount of COP 8 788 million in turnover (around USD 3 million or EUR 2.7 million) to accredit themselves within the SGSSS (including an additional capital of COP 965 million (around USD 330 000 or EUR 300 000). The decree also clarifies that resources for health care should be used for health care activities exclusively. This decree may imply a further reduction in number of EPS, as poorer performing EPS are absorbed by stronger ones. A further reduction in the number of EPS is expected to improve quality and efficiency, but will need to be balanced against the need to retain a sufficient number to enable user-choice and competition (both of which were important principles underpinning the 1993 reforms).

Health care service providers compete in a mixed public/private market

In 2010, there were approximately 46 300 health care providers in Colombia (Guerrero et al., 2011). Out of these, around 10 400 were *Instituciones Prestadoras de Salud* (IPS; 9 277 private and 1 113 public), whereas 35 000 were independent professionals, 341 were special transport services (ambulance) and 694 had a different function. There has been a growth in the number of private providers relative to public providers in recent years, although in more remote areas such as Chocó, the market remains dominated by public providers. The 1993 reforms established a purchaser-provider split, where public and private IPS are selectively contracted by EPS to provide health care services, in a managed competition model. Together, health facilities in Colombia provided 1.5 hospital beds per 1 000 inhabitants in 2013, around one-third of the OECD average of 4.8 beds per 1 000.

The quality assurance, monitoring and improvement framework applied to IPS is the same, whether they are in the public or private sector (and is discussed more fully in Chapter 2). The financial regulatory framework, however, depends upon the provider's public or private status. Private hospitals are subject to the usual regulatory framework applying to all commercial entities, while public hospitals have the status of a state-owned enterprise. Finances in the public sector appear poorly controlled, however. The operational deficit of public hospitals reached COP 160 591 million (around USD 55 million or EUR 50 million) in 2012, (Supersalud, 2014).

Part of the reason for this deficit may have been underfunding of public hospitals relative to need (particularly as enrolment in the SR expanded rapidly from 2002 onward, see Figure 1.7). There have also been complaints that EPS are slow to reimburse IPS, jeopardising their ability to invest and plan. A 2007 law states that EPS should reimburse at least 50% of costs to IPS within five days of an invoice (or 100% within one month for capitation-based contracts), but these requirements are often not adhered to. The findings of one study examining the finances and operations of 336 public hospitals between 2003 and 2011, however, also suggest that some of this deficit may be explained due to lack of investment in technology, leading to productivity losses (Orozco, 2014).

A number of proposals have been put forward to contain the problem of public hospital debt. More generous capitation payments in the SR (dating from 2011, see Figure 1.19), should provide some relief. Addressing Colombia's high rates of informality, and enabling more individuals to transfer to the CR, will also help. Clearly, however, increased funding should not be the only answer; reforms to reduce waste and improve productivity are also needed (a topic considered in depth in Chapter 2). A number of such reforms are currently being considered, including reforms to the way senior management teams are appointed, more demanding performance management frameworks (including pay-for-performance), and extension of public-private partnerships.

Public-private partnerships (PPP) are growing in importance. PPP are seen as a potential means to improve public sector performance, through greater use of innovative performance-related contracting with providers or workforce, for example. They are also seen as an opportunity to expand capacity and invest in infrastructure development. One recent study identified 21 cases of PPP in Colombia's health system, grouping these into three models (KPMG, 2015):

- ***Integral with one operator (contracts by Social State Agencies).*** The Social State Agency is responsible for complying with the hospital's obligations. The private operator is in charge of infrastructure, maintenance of facilities, it has some investment obligations and it provides all the clinical services.
- ***Integral with several operators (contracts by Social State Agencies).*** The Social State Agency has the obligation to co-ordinate the provision of all the services and they are responsible for complying with the hospital's obligations. The private operators provide the health care services and/or clinical support and they have some investment obligations.
- ***Integral with one operator (without Social State Agencies).*** Contracts are handled by the territorial entity. The private operator maintain the facilities and provide all the clinical services, it handles the infrastructure and has some investment obligations.

Challenges in optimising the regulatory framework around PPP remain however, in order to fully harness the potential benefits of private sector capacity and private sector approaches, whilst prioritising core health system values of access, equity and quality. In particular, the extent to which PPP may provide a solution to the problem of under-capacity (or poor quality and efficiency) in rural and remote areas remains unclear.

Colombia has very few doctors and nurses compared to OECD averages

Compared to OECD health systems, Colombia has very few doctors and nurses. Physician density in Colombia is 1.77 per 1 000 inhabitants, similar to Turkey but well below the OECD average of 3.27 (Figure 1.14). Colombia's nursing workforce causes even greater concern. On average, there are three times as many nurses as doctors in OECD health systems. This is not the case in Colombia. There, the density of nurses is 1.03 per 1 000 population, less than the density of physicians, and almost a tenth of the OECD average density of 9.09 (Figure 1.15). Workforce density is much lower in rural areas. Some remote and small municipalities depend on one physician per 10 000, or more, inhabitants.

Figure 1.14. Practising physicians per 1 000 population in 2013

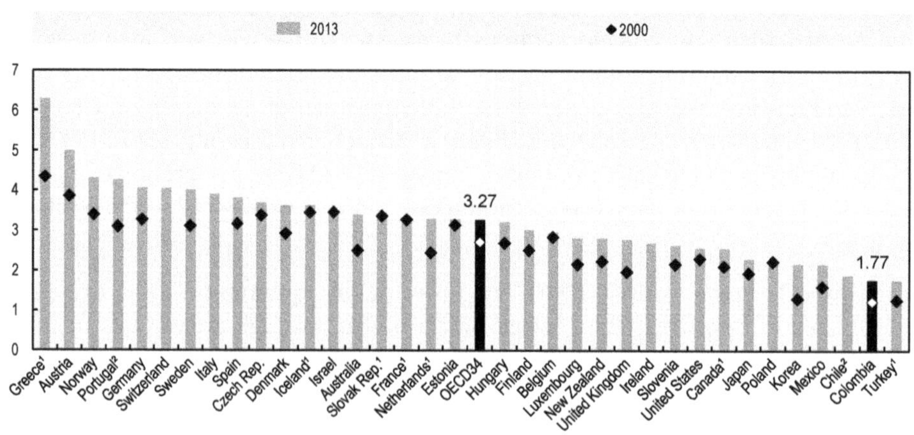

1. Data include not only doctors providing direct care to patients, but also those working in the health sector as managers, educators, researchers, etc. (adding *another* 5-10% of doctors). 2. Data refer to all doctors licensed to practice (resulting in a large over-estimation of the number of practising doctors in Portugal, of around 30%).

Source: *OECD Health Statistics 2015*, http://dx.doi.org/ 10.1787/health-data-en.

Figure 1.15. Practising nurses per 1 000 population in 2013

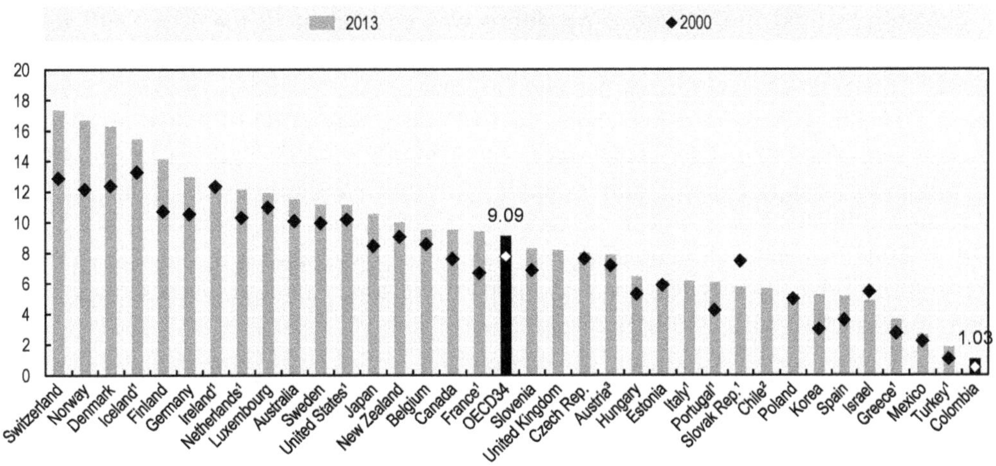

1. Data include not only nurses providing direct care to patients, but also those working in the health sector as managers, educators, researchers, etc. 2. Data in Chile refer to all nurses who are licensed to practice (less than one-third are professional nurses with a university degree). 3. Austria reports only nurses employed in hospital.

Source: OECD Health Statistics 2015, http://dx.doi.org/ 10.1787/health-data-en.

Addressing Colombia's workforce shortage will require attention to some fundamental issues. It was agreed in 2010 that both the MSPS and the Ministry of Education would carry out joint evaluations of health-related undergraduate and post-graduate programmes. A full evaluation is carried out in order to accredit the training programme. For renewal of approved status, only service and teaching conditions are monitored. Nevertheless, only 10% of the nearly 45 000 students enrolled to study medicine in the past decade have actually graduated, showing that there is room for greater efficiency and quality controls.

A lack of strategic vision also characterises management of the post-graduate workforce. Many doctors (especially in primary care) have short contracts of less than a year, meaning there is little incentive for the doctor and his or her employer to mutually invest and maximise the doctor's contribution. Residents must fund their own specialist training, meaning that specialities that are less lucrative in the long term (such as primary care) are less attractive than other careers, such as the surgical specialities with a high volume of private work. Training numbers within each speciality are decided by professional associations, and not by the MSPS, which again implies a lack of strategic co-ordination.

The number of women training in medicine in Colombia is now equal to men. Although this is a welcomed achievement, it does imply a need for improved contractual conditions and workforce flexibility in the future.

1.5. Systems to raise and distribute health care resources

Health system funding comes from a variety of sources. These are mainly employee and employer payroll contributions for the contributory regime (CR); and national and local tax revenues, as well as cross-subsidisation from the CR in the case of the subsidised regime (SR). This section describes in better detail how revenues are raised and how health care services are purchased and managed.

Spending on health care is low in Colombia compared to OECD averages

Colombia's total health care expenditure was equivalent to 6.8% of GDP in 2013, positioning the country well below the OECD average of 8.9% (see Figure 2.4 in Chapter 2). Health expenditure in per capita terms is even further away from the OECD average. Health expenditure per capita in Colombia was USD PPP 864 in 2013, four times lower than the OECD average of USD PPP 3 453 (Figure 1.16), although differences in local prices are likely to explain a significant proportion of this difference. Spending on health has however increased in recent years, having risen from 5.4% of GDP in 2004. Much of this increase was due to the expenditure in the CR. Growth in expenditure in the SR was less than one half of the total increase, even though it has a larger number of affiliates (MSPS, 2013a).

Figure 1.16. Health expenditure per capita in 2013

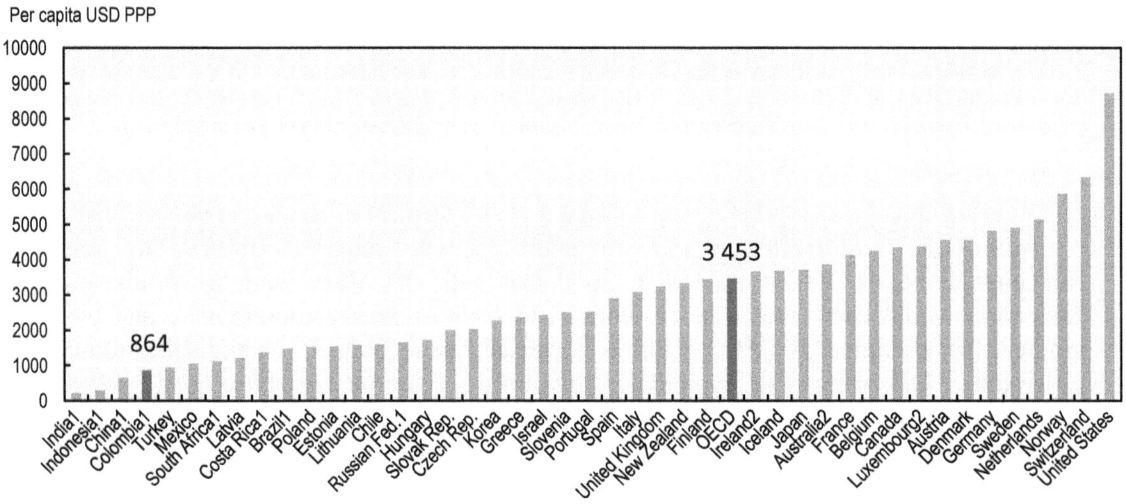

1. Includes investments.

2. Data refers to 2012.

Source: *OECD Health Statistics 2015*, http://dx.doi.org/ 10.1787/health-data-en.

In 2010, public spending corresponded to 80.5% of total health spending, placing Colombia on a level similar to many OECD countries. As a share of total health care costs, the out-of-pocket (OOP) expenditure is 15%. The sustained reduction of OOP expenditure is one of the greatest achievements of the Colombian health care system after the promulgation of Law 100 in 1993. OOP expenditure on health is today mainly due to charges related to consultations (23%), medication (10.2%) and procedures (14.9%).

Revenues are raised from multiple public and private sources

Funding in the SGSSS involves more than ten different sources, as well as multiple actors responsible for the collection and management of resources (Nuñez, 2012). For the CR, the main sources for financing include obligatory contributions for employers and employees to the CR (42.3%) (12.5% of the employee's salary goes to FOSYGA; 8% is paid by the employer and 4.5% is paid by the employee), financial resources from general taxes (20.4%) and out-of-pocket expenditure (21.3%). These revenues are collected in a fund called *Fondo de Solidaridad y Garantia* (FOSYGA). The FOSYGA redistributes pooled funds to each EPS on a capitation basis. The basic per capita transfer is known as the *Unidad de Pago por Capitación* (UPC), although overall EPS income is adjusted for age, sex and region. EPS also obtain other income by payment from the users, "co-pays" (Procuraduría, 2012).

The FOSYGA also has a solidarity function; in that it transfers some resources to the solidarity subaccount for the SR. Revenues to the solidarity subaccount are also raised from contributions from the national budget, oil exports and from the social aggregated value tax. The solidarity subaccount of the FOSYGA then transfers funds to the municipalities and departments. In turn, these local authorities also raise funds from local taxes, thus pooling funds together for allowing to contract with EPS serving the SR.

Funds are redistributed to EPS through a risk-adjusted capitation formula

EPS receive their revenues through the *Unidad de Pago por Capitación* (Capitated Payment Unit, UPC) per enrollee, with some adjustment for geographic, demographic and – to a lesser extent – epidemiologic factors. In the early years of the SGSSS, the UPC was calculated on the basis of available funds (prioritising solvency rather than meeting health care needs), and was more generous in the CR compared to the SR. Later, this approach has evolved to place greater weight on meeting health care needs. The UPC is now calculated on an actuarial basis, estimating likely demand for services included in the POS given the underlying demographic and epidemiologic profile. With equalisation of the benefits basket included in the CR and SR (announced in 2012), in recent years the UPC in the SR has caught up with that of the CR (Figure 1.17). It is projected that as of 2015, there will be no difference in the capitation payments in each regime.

Figure 1.17. Capitation Payment Unit for the contributory (UPC-C) and subsidised (UPC-S) regimes between 1994 and 2013, in Colombian pesos

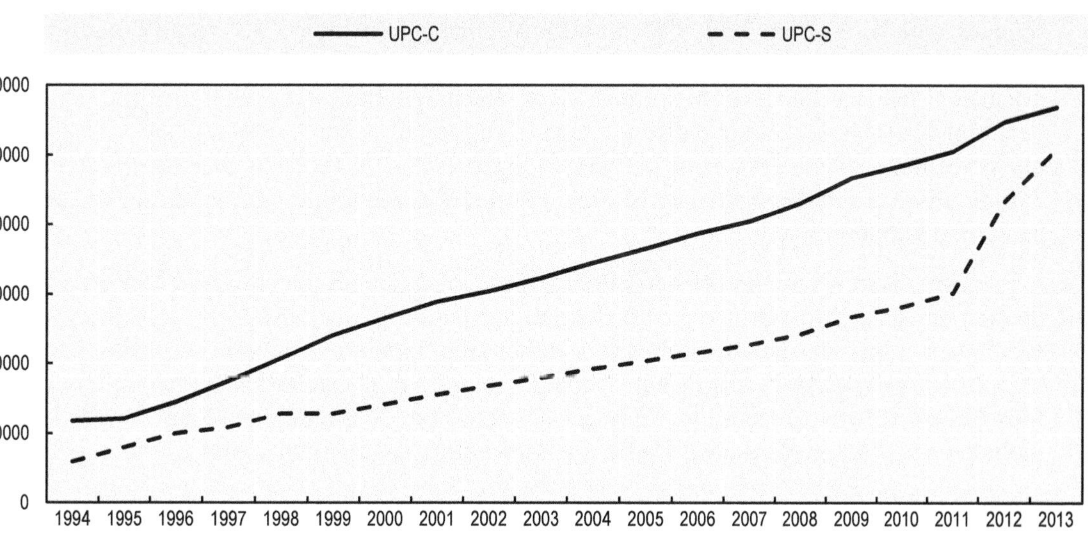

Source: Así vamos en salud (2012), www.asivamosensalud.org/inidicadores/financiamiento/grafica.ver/46.

Contracting for services is not as innovative as it could be

EPS have substantial freedom to contract with IPS in whichever way they wish – whether via capitation, fee-for-service, block contracts for pre-specified volumes of activity, or block-contracts for pre-specified groups of patients with defined needs (similar to the diagnosis-related group, or DRG, system used in many OECD countries). Outcomes-based contracting (through pay-for-performance, or payment-by-results) is also permitted. However, little use is made of more innovative contracting models, especially in the SR. For services of low complexity (e.g. primary care), the usual contracting model is based on capitation. For services of medium to high complexity, the usual contracting model is fee-for-service, although block-contracts for pre-specified volumes of activity are also widely used. These contracting models do not contain strong incentives to improve quality or efficiency.

One tool that EPS do have available to encourage efficiency is freedom to negotiate price. There are, currently, very few national price tariffs in use in Colombia. The exception to this are regulated tariffs for emergency care following road accidents (known as the *Seguro Obligatorio de Accidentes de Tránsito*, or SOAT system; developed so that individuals could be assured of prompt care in any IPS following a road accident, without anxiety over whether their EPS would cover costs). SOAT tariffs are used as a reference point in negotiations for other types of care – but, in practice the price difference in a procedure such as endoscopy can be much higher depending on the provider.

An important factor holding back the development of more innovative contracting models, geared to incentivising quality and productivity, is the lack of reliable information on the activities, costs and outcomes in the IPS sector. As Colombia's health system information infrastructure becomes better developed (see Section 1.6), greater opportunities to contract for quality, outcomes and value should present themselves. The MSPS is keen to see wider use of pay-for-performance schemes. A pilot scheme, around the management of patients with renal chronic diseases, started in 2014. This is a national scheme with EPS from both CR and SR regimes, in which EPS receive additional resources for treating not only patients with renal chronic diseases but also patients with precursor diseases (such as hypertension or diabetes). Indicators used in this pay-for-performance scheme include the percentage of registered patients with precursor diseases, the percentage of patients with precursor diseases that have been examined for renal chronic disease and the incidence of renal chronic disease at the later stages of the pilot, compared with baseline.

Another area where quality and outcomes are inadequately incentivised concerns how doctors are paid. Most primary care doctors are paid a salary, and most secondary care specialists earn via fees-for-service. Neither reimbursement model contains strong incentives for quality or efficiency (indeed, salaries may encourage underactivity and fees-for-service may incentivise unnecessary activity). To date, few EPS or IPS have included a pay-for-performance element in their reimbursement packages for doctors.

Procurement practices are also showing more innovation, particularly for pharmaceuticals

Colombia has made impressive progress in controlling the prices paid for pharmaceuticals. Medication costs were a serious problem until 2012, because no adequate regulation about costs was in place. As a result, the price of medications in Colombia could reach three or four times prices in the rest of the world (DNP, 2012). Reforms in 2013 (described in Box 1.4), however, successfully established maximum prices for pharmaceuticals. To date, the price of 863 pharmaceuticals has been regulated through the new pricing mechanism, 585 of which are included in the POS. This has resulted in a 42% average reduction of prices, saving around USD 180 million.

The success of controlling prices in the pharmaceutical sector has not been matched by similar successes in other sectors. There are, however, proposals to apply a similar approach to determine prices for medical devices. For coronary stents, there are already price control mechanisms in place, with plans to extend such mechanisms to other high-cost devices. Given the variable nature of medical devices' markets, the MSPS is likely to apply different methodologies for different devices.

Box 1.4. Pharmaceutical price regulation

Until 2012, the cost of medications in Colombia was not regulated – and as a consequence, both providers and insurance companies increased their price. Prices climbed further through the use of *tutelas* whereby the FOSYGA was effectively required to sign a blank check for any approved claim (Bardey, 2013). In 2012, a new national pharmaceutical policy was launched. It included ten strategies to improve accessibility, and quality of pharmaceuticals, in order to better meet population health care needs, irrespective of individuals' ability to pay (CONPES, 2012). The policy aimed to establish methods to identify the medicines that should be subject to price control and determine their highest sale price.

In 2014, another decree relevant to biopharmaceuticals (including monoclonal antibodies and other immunotherapies) was issued. Although these pharmaceuticals comprise only 1% of product registrations in Colombia, they represent up to 30% of national pharmaceutical expenditure (COP 2 billion annually, around USD 690 000 or EUR 629 000). This is likely to increase, in line with global trends. It is estimated, however, that prices could fall by between 30 and 60% if price controls and/or more competitive market conditions were in place.

1.6. Information systems underpinning health care delivery

Health system information in Colombia has, historically, been characterised by a focus on inputs and activities, with much less information on outcomes or costs. The government has however made increasing efforts to create a relevant digital platform and, with that, the MSPS has established the Strategic Plan for Information Technology and Communications that aims to add value from technological resources in the health system through the development of digital registers and systems for sharing information. This section reviews the way Colombia is building its information infrastructure to monitor health care activities, costs and quality.

SISPRO is an initiative to consolidate all health and social care information into a single data-warehouse

The health care sector in Colombia is comprised of several information systems. Until recently, these disparate systems were poorly integrated. In recent years, however, the Colombian Government has made great efforts to create a relevant digital platform to increase the use of information technologies, electronic registers and communications through a strategy called *Gobierno En Linea* (GEL, or on-line government). This national strategy is managed by the Ministry of Information Technologies and Communication and intends to cover all services rendered by the government. In particular, GEL has specific components related to the health sector, which are managed by the MSPS and materialised in the *Sistema Integral de Información de la Protección Social* (Integral System for Information in Social Protection, SISPRO).

SISPRO is a data warehouse for services and care provided across the Colombian health care system. It brings together several databases that cover financing and health accounts; individuals' health care needs, risk factors and service utilisation; distribution and characteristics of insurers; and, distribution and characteristics of providers, including some indicators of quality and outcomes. SISPRO is administered by the MSPS and it integrates information on four elements: health, pensions, labour risks and social promotion (employment and social assistance). Each component of the system has an independent reporting and consolidation structure. Key components, from the health system perspective, include a register of individuals affiliated the health system (RUAF, or the *Registro Único de Afiliados*), each with a unique-identifier which allows linkage of records; a register of people with incapacities; a register of health care providers (RIPS, or the *Registro Individual de Prestación de Servicios de Salud*); an information system on prices of medicines (SISMED, or the *Sistema de Medicamentos*); and an information system on public hospitals' activities and spending (SIHO, or the *Sistema de Información Hospitalaria*).

In addition to the information registers, SISPRO co-ordinates observatories that provide analyses of population health care need (*Análisis de la sitación de salud*, ASIS). It also incorporates tools to analyse socio-economic inequalities in health. Data can be disaggregated by region or municipality, gender, age and several other characteristics of the population under analysis. Once fully operational, SISPRO is intended to support health system monitoring and planning, as well as providing public access to key health system statistics and reports. Its website (sispro.gov.co) already allows users to construct search queries on insurance coverage, service use and high-level outcomes such as mortality.

In all, MSPS co-ordinates 30 registers or observatories covering a broad variety of topics including HIV/AIDS; mental health; maternal health; teenage pregnancy; aging; disability; ethnic groups; food security and nutrition; cancer; chronic diseases (diabetes mellitus, chronic renal disease, cardiovascular disease); gender-based violence; zoonotic infections; inequalities and health equity. The National Cancer Information System is an example of how IT and communications have been used to develop a comprehensive register that contains information on mortality, incidence, service provision and inequality at a national and local level.

In addition, SIVIGILA is an event reporting system of interest for public health, administered by the National Health Institute, and reports specific infectious diseases. The National Liaison Centre uses the information produced by SIVIGILA for informing international organisations of any threat to public health. Finally, SISMED is an information system built to provide the data needed to analyse and control the behaviour of prices of drugs in Colombia and thus orient the authorities to enable informed policymaking regarding the regulation of the pharmaceutical market in the country.

Public reporting of health care quality and outcomes is improving

As part of SISPRO, the *Observatorio de Calidad* (or Observatory for Health Care Quality, calidadensalud.minsalud.gov.co) has been established to provide information on the quality of care to users, members of the SGSSS, health practitioners, academics and the general public, within three dimensions: quality of services; respect of the rights of users; and health outcomes and results (Table 1.1). This tool aims to contribute to improve the performance of health care providers and provide information to the user to support informed choice of provider. As of 2013, information for 37 indicators of access in primary care, technical grade, risk management and customer satisfaction for IPS and EPS were available.

The quality of services is assessed by questionnaires containing 14 questions, where users are asked to rate service by the EPS. The dimension respect of rights of users is assessed through indicators measuring aspects related to the denial of services, lack of timely provision of services, unnecessary procedures, poorly co-ordinated care, barriers to affiliation and denial of services where authorised by a physician. Finally, the dimension of health outcomes and results gathers information about quality of medical appointments (general, specialised and dental), maternal and infant health (low birth weight and infant and maternal health), communicable diseases (treatment of people with HIV) and chronical diseases (management of arterial hypertension). Each entity is responsible for reporting the information to the National Health Superintendence. After receiving and validating the information, the National Health Superintendence is in charge of sending it to the MSPS, who will then make it publicly available through its website.

Table 1.1. Performance indicators monitored by the Observatory for Health Care Quality

Category	IPS Indicators	EPS Indicators
Accessibility and opportunity in primary care	Timeliness in the scheduling of general medicine consultation	Timeliness in the scheduling of general medicine consultation
	Timeliness in the scheduling of specialist consultation	Timeliness in the scheduling of specialist consultation
	Timeliness in the scheduling of internal medicine consultation	Timeliness in the scheduling of internal medicine consultation
	Timeliness in the scheduling of gynaecologic consultation	Timeliness in the scheduling of gynaecologic consultation
	Timeliness in the scheduling of paediatric consultation	Timeliness in the scheduling of paediatric consultation
	Timeliness in the scheduling of general surgery consultation	Number of tutelas for failing to provide services
	Opportunity in the scheduling of diagnosis exams	Timeliness in the provision of POS medicines
	Share of cancelled programmed surgeries	Timeliness in performing scheduled surgery
	Timeliness in emergency care	Timeliness in the scheduling of orthodontic consultation
	Timeliness in imaging services	Timeliness in imaging services
	Timeliness in general orthodontic care	Timeliness in the scheduling of general surgery consultation
	Timeliness in scheduled surgery care	Timeliness in the referral to EAPB
Technical grade	Readmission rate of hospitalised patients	Share of successful vaccination programmes for children under 1 year old
	Share of controlled patients with hypertension	Timeliness in the detection of cervical cancer
Risk management	Hospital mortality rate after 48 hours	Maternal mortality rate
	Hospital infection rate Monitoring of adverse events	Pneumonia mortality rate for high risk population groups
Customer experience	General satisfaction rate	General satisfaction rate Share of complaints resolved in under 15 days Rate of transfers from the EAPB

Source: Ministry of Health and Social Protection.

The SOGSC's monitoring allows comparison of the performances of individual IPS and EPS – as well as comparison of municipal, departmental or country averages. The general satisfaction rate with the IPS in Colombia was for example 87.5% in 2012, with differences from 62.5% in the department of Santander to 97.93% in Putumayo (Figure 1.18).

Figure 1.18. Satisfaction rates with health care providers, by department, 2012

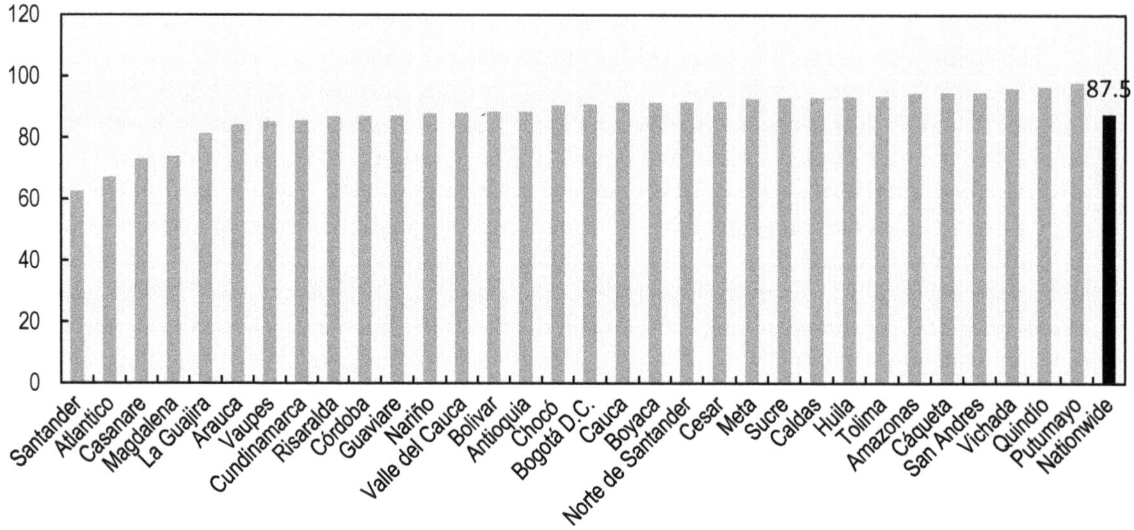

Note: No data available for Guanía in 2012

Source: Observatory for Health Care Quality, Ministry of Health and Social Protection.

Data gathered from Colombia's decentralised health system has thus improved – but further work is needed in order to bring together and support national information infrastructure and capacity for data use at a country level. To be useful for the assessment of progress in population health and the quality of care, health and health care data collections need to be further organised in a systematic and efficient way, to be structured to support linkage across data sources, as well as to be publicly accessible.

Use of electronic records and tele-health is under developed

Use of electronic health records in Colombia appears to be limited. In a survey carried out in 2014, only 35% of service providers reported that they gathered, stored and transmitted information with a certain degree of automation; whereas over 46% still relied on paper records. Service providers that also provide tele-health are much more likely to manage information digitally: 77% of providers without tele-health use paper records, while only one out of three providers that offers tele-health stores information in this modality. Private providers are more likely to handle information with a certain degree of automation than public providers (see Table 1.2).

Table 1.2. State of information management by provider type

Handling of patients' records	Private provider	Public provider	Total
Some automation	94	170	264
Paper only	72	273	345
No data	30	109	139
Automation rate	48%	31%	35%
Total	**196**	**552**	**748**

Source: Ministry of Health and Social Protection.

Regional differences are apparent. In the Andean region, for example, more than half of service providers have some form of electronic record keeping. In the North coast area, the number decreases to less than half. Of particular note, in poor and rural departments such as Amazonas and Caquetá, the degree of electronic record keeping is almost non-existent. Lack of IT infrastructure in these departments is likely to significantly impede telemedicine and other IT-based initiatives to overcome the challenges of physical remoteness.

The transfer of digital patient records and other health service information is enabled by the Individual Register of Health Service Provision (RIPS). There is a number of mandatory statistics that need to be reported to the public authorities by primary care physicians, hospitals and clinics and local and central government. Taking the medical records and the service provision receipts as basic sources; the information shared includes identification of involved stakeholders (EPS, IPS, user), services (such as diagnostic or therapeutic procedures) and patients' originating health care need. Patient data being transferred and stored electronically is regulated by RIPS, in accordance to Resolution 3084 of 2000.This information exchange system is the minimum data set that the SGSSS requires for management, regulation and control processes. The data identify health activities undertaken by IPS or independent health professionals and enable the development of epidemiologic profiles, frequency of use and cost of services, met and unmet health care needs, and contract monitoring.

1.7. Conclusions

Many measures of health system performance in Colombia have improved since Law 100 created the *Sistema General de Seguridad Social en Salud* in 1993. Close to 100% of the population belong to a health insurance scheme, with equal benefits and equal per capita funding irrespective of employment status. Out-of-pocket payments represent around 15% of total national health expenditure (equivalent to around 1% of GDP), one of the lowest levels in Latin America and even lower than the OECD average.

Many indicators, such as affiliation rates to the SGSSS, increases in service use and reductions in unmet health care needs, have improved most rapidly in low income and rural populations, demonstrating the strongly progressive nature of the reforms. Significant geographical differences in the density of health care facilities and workforce persist, however. Poor employment contracts, inefficient payment systems that reward activity and not outcomes, and a lack of quality-related infrastructure, also mean that the health care sector in Colombia is not performing as well as it could.

In broad terms, health care insurers and health care providers are not as developed as they need to be to deliver a high-quality, efficient and sustainable health care system – issues considered in detail in the following chapter.

Notes

1. P90/P10 represents the ratio of the upper bound of the ninth income decile (i.e. the 10% of people with highest income) to that of the first decile (i.e. the 10% of people with lowest income).

2. The Gini Coefficient measures the inequality across levels of income. A Gini coefficient of zero expresses perfect equality, where everyone has the same income). A Gini coefficient of one (or 100%) expresses maximal inequality (where only one person has all the income and all others have none).

References

Así vamos en salud (2012) www.asivamosensalud.org/inidicadores/financiamiento/grafica.ver/46.

Banco de la República (2006), "La economía Colombiana: Situación actual frente a los noventas", www.banrep.gov.co/docum/ftp/borra429.pdf.

Bardey, D. (2013), "Los precios de los medicamentos en Colombia", http://lasillavacia.com/elblogueo/blog/los-precios-de-los-medicamentos-en-colombia-por-david-bardey.

Barón, G. (2014), "Cuentas de Salud de Colombia 2004-2013", Ministerio de Salud y Protección Social, Bogotá.

Bernal, O. and C. Gutierrez (2012), *La salud en Colombia, logros, retos y recomendaciones*, Editorial Universidad de Los Andes.

Bernal, O. and D. Zamora (2014), "A Better Understanding of Reasons for the Failure of the Health care Reform in Colombia", *Health*, Vol. 06, No. 21, pp. 2918–2926, http://dx.doi.org/10.4236/health.2014.621330.

BID – Banco Interamericano de. Desarrollo (2010), "Crimen e inseguridad, indicadores para las Americas", www.oas.org/dsp/FLACSO/flacso_inseguridad.pdf.

CONPES – Consejo Nacional de Política Económica y Social (2012), "Politica Farmaceutica Nacional", www.minsalud.gov.co/Documentos y Publicaciones/Politica Farmacéutica Nacional.pdf.

Contraloría (2013), "Función de Advertencia. Gastos de Administración Intervención Saludcoop EPS", www.contraloria.gov.co/documents/10136/79192176/FA_2013EE0119319-Gastos-Admon-Intervencion-Saludcoop-EPS-04102013.pdf/c99dfbec-d0d1-404c-a3f5-011a264cf811.

Corte Constitucional (2013), "Sentencia C-262/13", www.corteconstitucional.gov.co/relatoria/2013/C-262-13.htm.

DANE – National Statistics Authority (2013), "Medición del empleo informal y seguridad social", www.dane.gov.co/files/investigaciones/boletines/ech/ech_informalidad/re_ech_informalidad_mar_may2013.pdf.

DANE (2011a), "Colombia, Necesidades Básicas Insatisfechas – NBI, por total, cabecera y resto, según municipio y nacional", www.dane.gov.co/files/censos/resultados/NBI_total_municipios_30_Jun_2011.pdf.

DANE (2011b), "Encuesta de Calidad de Vida (Life Quality Survey)", www.dane.gov.co/index.php/esp/estadisticas-sociales/calidad-de-vida-ecv/87-sociales/calidad-de-vida/3281-encuesta-de-calidad-de-vida-2011.

DANE (2008), "Proyecciones poblacionales 2006-2020", www.dane.gov.co/files/investigaciones/poblacion/proyepobla06_20/MProyeccionesMunicipalesedadsexo.pdf.

DANE (2007), "Colombia, una nación Multicultural", www.dane.gov.co/files/censo2005/etnia/sys/colombia_nacion.pdf.

DNP – Departamento Nacional de Planeación (2012), "Política Farmaceútica Nacional", www.minsalud.gov.co/Documentos%20y%20Publicaciones/Politica%20Farmacéutica%20Nacional.pdf.

Finol, K. (2014), "Radiografía de la oferta de servicios de salud en Colombia", Banco de la República, Economía Regional, www.banrep.gov.co/sites/default/files/publicaciones/archivos/dtser_202.pdf.

Gaviria, A. (2013), "Los puntos claves de la reforma en salud", www.eltiempo.com/archivo/documento/CMS-12615423.

Guerrero, R. et al. (2011), "Sistema de salud de Colombia", www.scielosp.org/pdf/spm/v53s2/10.pdf.

Guzman, K. (2014), "Radiografía de la oferta de servicios de salud en Colombia", Tomado de www.banrep.gov.co/docum/Lectura_finanzas/pdf/dtser_202.pdf.

ICRC – International Committee of the Red Cross (2011), "Informe de actividades Colombia 2011 – situación humanitaria", www.icrc.org/spa/resources/documents/feature/2012/colombia-report-2012-04-18.htm.

IHME – Institute for Health Metrics and Evaluation (2014), "GDP Profile: Colombia", www.healthdata.org/sites/default/files/files/country_profiles/GBD/ihme_gbd_country_report_colombia.pdf.

Javeriana (2014), "Estimación de la carga de enfermedad para Colombia, 2010", www.javeriana.edu.co/documents/12789/4434885/Carga+de+Enfermedad+Colombia+2010.pdf/e0dbfe7b-40a2-49cb-848e-bd67bf7bc62e.

MSPS – Ministry of Health and Social Protection (2013a), "Análisis de Situación de Salud según regiones: Colombia", www.MSPS.gov.co/Documentos%20y%20Publicaciones/An%C3%A1lisis%20de%20situaci%C3%B3n%20de%20salud%20por%20regiones.pdf.

MSPS (2013b), "Plan Decenal de Salud Pública 2012-2021", www.MSPS.gov.co/Documentos%20y%20Publicaciones/Plan%20Decenal%20-%20Documento%20en%20consulta%20para%20aprobaci%C3%B3n.pdf.

MSPS (2014a), "Mortalidad evitable en Colombia 1998-2011", Observatorio Nacional de Salud, www.ins.gov.co/lineas-de-accion/ons/SiteAssets/Paginas/publicaciones/Informe3-ME-ONS-Definitivo.pdf.

MSPS (2014b), "Análisis de Situación de Salud Colombia 2013", www.minsalud.gov.co/sites/rid/Lists/BibliotecaDigital/RIDE/VS/ED/PSP/ASIS%2024022014.pdf.

MSPS (2014c), "Decreto 1782 del 2014", Biotecnológicos, www.minsalud.gov.co/Normatividad_Nuevo/Decreto%201782%20de%202014.pdf.

MSPS (2014d), "Decreto 2702 del 2014", www.achc.org.co/documentos/afiliados/Decretos/DECRETO%202702%20DEL%2023%20DE%20DICIEMBRE%20DE%202014%20-%20HABILITACION%20EPS.pdf.

Nuñez, J. et al. (2012), "La sostenibilidad financiera del sistema de salud colombiano: dinámica del gasto y principales retos de cara al futuro", Fundación para la Educación Superior y el Desarrollo.

Observatorio de Drogas de Colombia (2013). "Estudio nacional de consumo de sustancias psicoactivas en Colombia: Informe Final".

OECD (forthcoming), *OECD Reviews of Labour Market and Social Policies: Colombia*, OECD Publishing, Paris.

OECD (2015a), *OECD Health Statistics 2015*, http://dx.doi.org/ 10.1787/health-data-en.

OECD (2015b), *OECD Review of Agricultural Policies: Colombia 2015*, OECD Publishing, Paris, http://dx.doi.org/10.1787/9789264227644-en.

OECD (2015c), "Aggregate National Accounts, SNA 2008 (or SNA 1993): Gross domestic product", *OECD National Accounts Statistics* (database), http://dx.doi.org/10.1787/data-00001-en.

Orozco, A. (2014), "Una aproximación regional a la eficiencia y productividad de los hospitales públicos colombianos", www.banrep.gov.co/sites/default/files/publicaciones/archivos/dtser_201.pdf.

Orozco, A. (2006), "Por que reformar la reforma", http://www.eumed.net/libros-gratis/2006a/jmo/indice.htm.

Supersalud (2014), "Superintendencia de Salud", Bogotá, www.supersalud.gov.co.

UNDP – United Nations Development Programme (2014), "United Nations Human Development Report 2014", http://hdr.undp.org/sites/default/files/hdr14-report-en-1.pdf.

UNHCR – United Nations High Commissioner for Refugees (2011), "Desplazamiento forzado, tierras y territorios", www.acnur.org/t3/fileadmin/scripts/doc.php?file=biblioteca/pdf/7599.

Velasco, N. et al. (2013), "The judicialization of Health in Colombia", Edis, Publishing Institution of the University of Zilina Univerzitná.

WHO (2014), "Colombia", www.who.int/nmh/countries/col_en.pdf.

World Bank (2015a), "Fertility rate, total (births per woman)", http://data.worldbank.org/indicator/SP.DYN.TFRT.IN.

World Bank (2015b), "Tasa de incidencia de la pobreza, sobre la base de la línea de pobreza nacional (% de la población)", http://datos.bancomundial.org/indicador/SI.POV.NAHC/countries/CO?display=graph.

World Bank (2015c), "GINI index (World Bank estimates)", http://data.worldbank.org/indicator/SI.POV.GINI.

Database references

OECD Health Statistics, http://dx.doi.org/ 10.1787/health-data-en.

OECD National Accounts Statistics, http://dx.doi.org/10.1787/data-00001-en.

OECD Social and Welfare Statistics, http://dx.doi.org/10.1787/data-00654-en.

WHO Global Health Expenditure Database, http://apps.who.int/nha/database.

Chapter 2

Performance of the Colombian health system

Over the last 20 years, Colombia has achieved remarkable improvements in access to health care services for disadvantaged populations, while reducing out-of-pocket payments as a source of health care financing, with likely positive implications for overall levels of financial protection. However, in spite of its recent achievements, the Colombian health sector faces important challenges to maintain and improve current performance levels.

A key weakness is that insurance agencies are not adequately fulfilling their role to manage both clinical and financial risk in the system. A lack of informational and financial incentives means that the envisaged model of managed competition between payers has not convincingly materialised in practice, holding back improvements in quality and efficiency. Although Colombia is taking steps, more will need to be done to build a more demanding performance framework around both insurers and health care providers.

The statistical data for Israel are supplied by and under the responsibility of the relevant Israeli authorities. The use of such data by the OECD is without prejudice to the status of the Golan Heights, East Jerusalem and Israeli settlements in the West Bank under the terms of international law.

2.1. Introduction

Colombia has achieved great progress in terms of formal health coverage – measured by enrolment into a formal health insurance scheme – since the reforms started in 1993. Recent data indicate that about 96% of Colombians are now covered by health insurance arrangements. Progress in formal coverage has been accompanied by remarkable improvements over the last 20 years in access to services by disadvantaged populations and increased health sector funding, while reducing the participation of out-of-pocket payments as a source of health care financing, with likely positive implications for overall levels of financial protection.

Despite its recent achievements, the Colombian health sector faces important challenges to maintain and improve current performance levels. Some of these challenges are common to countries at similar stages of economic development as Colombia, including a rapidly ageing population and declining workforce. Other challenges arise from the specific way the country's health system and its institutions were reorganised in 1993 and the subsequent adjustments made since then. To name but a few, improvements in health care access and outcomes have not been equally distributed across geographic regions and socio-economic groups, and the envisaged model of managed competition between payers has not much materialised in practice, creating weak incentives for care quality enhancing activities at the provider level.

This chapter explores steps Colombia could take in order to refocus health system priorities towards improved performance, both in terms of efficiency and quality of care. Specifically, a set of policy strategies is presented, based on the experience of other countries that have faced similar challenges to Colombia. Such policy strategies involve changes to how the roles of purchaser, provider and oversight are currently organised, how the purchasing of goods and services and provider reimbursement occur, and how the health system information infrastructure is set up.

This chapter provides an overview of the main challenges to the Colombian health system in particular areas, followed by a section suggesting policy priorities to enhance both efficiency and quality in the system. Some of these policy alternatives are identified in the light of international experiences in the OECD and elsewhere, and their feasibility assessed specifically in the Colombian context.

Section 2.2 outlines some of the main challenges lying ahead concerning access to care and related equity issues. Section 2.3 presents issues around quality of health care provision, whilst Section 2.4 deals with heightened concerns in Colombia about the health system's financial sustainability. Pressing efficiency aspects in the health system are discussed in Section 2.5. Finally, Section 2.6 identifies policy priorities for the Colombian Government with the aim of tackling the main challenges surrounding access to care, care quality, financial sustainability and efficiency. A summary of the main policy messages from this chapter concludes.

2.2. Access to care

Colombia's progress in enrolling its population to formal health insurance schemes has been remarkable over the last 20 years. This is mainly due to the expansion of the subsidised regime (SR), particularly after 2004. Figures for the year 2012 suggest an enrolment rate of 96% of the population to either the SR or the contributory regime (CR), with slightly higher population coverage for the former.

Inequalities in access have been addressed with considerable success

Data on health service utilisation indicate that in 2010 members of the CR demanded more services on average than their SR counterparts. A similar picture emerges if the comparison is made between people not living in poverty (defined as having no unmet basic needs) and those living in poverty/extreme poverty, with the former demanding more services on average. Access to services was good, or better, in the subsidised regime, however. According to the results of a national survey about EPS services conducted by the MSPS in 2014, the average of enrolees waiting more than ten days for consultation with a general doctor was 10.1% among EPS in the SR, compared to 13.3% among EPS in the CR. For specialist appointments, an average of 15.5% of enrolees waited more than 30 days among EPS in the SR, compared to 26.3% in the CR (MSPS, 2012).

Furthermore, unlike other countries of the region financial barriers to access such as out-of-pocket (OOP) payments appear to be less of an issue than the physical availability of services and professionals. The MSPS estimated that the share of OOP payments in Colombia was 15.2% of the funding of the health system in 2012 (as seen in Chapter 1). While the WHO estimated that the OOP in Colombia was somewhat higher (around 17%) in 2012, it was still among the lowest in Latin America (Figure 2.1) and also lower than the OECD average of around 20%.

Figure 2.1. Out-of-pocket expenditure in Colombia and other Latin American countries, 2012

Percentage of total expenditure on health

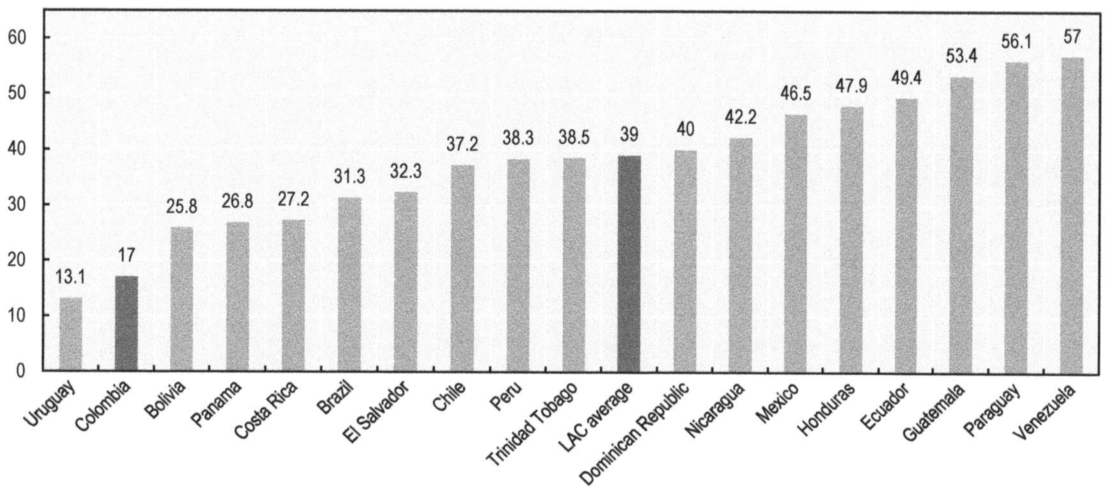

Note: The average for Latin America (LAC) includes those countries whose data are available for 2012, excluding Colombia.

Source: WHO (2015), "Out-of-pocket Expenditure as a Percentage of Total Expenditure on Health", http://apps.who.int/gho/data/node.imr.WHS7_150?lang=en.

A likely explanation for this success in controlling OOP spending is the modest magnitude of cost-sharing in the system, and relatively generous exemption rules. Cost-sharing is determined both by the scheme that the person belongs to and their assessed socio-economic vulnerability, measured by an index called SISBEN. Enrolees of the SR make no co-payments for services if they belong to SISBEN 1 (most vulnerable individuals) and pay only a 5% co-insurance rate if they belong to SISBEN 2. Members of the CR pay a flat fee for services which varies according to income levels, but again the magnitude of such fees tends to be relatively small.

Colombia must maintain its emphasis on pooled sources of health financing to keep decreasing the share of OOP payments in total health spending, which will be a fundamental source of continued improvements in financial protection for its citizens.

Access to health care through litigation is a prominent phenomenon, favouring the better-off

An important challenge to the Colombian health system has been the substantial growth of the mechanism of *tutelas*, a litigation measure whereby citizens may go to court to obtain access to health care services that they feel are being denied to them. With 81% of cases being approved by the Court at the first hearing, the number of *tutelas* has grown significantly, from 24 843 in 2000 to 117 746 in 2014, at an estimated cost of USD 14 billion between 2005 and 2014 (Rodriguez, 2010).

The fact that this mechanism has been increasingly used to grant access to services *included* in the POS can be interpreted as a signal that the timeliness and quality of care provided in the system have important shortcomings. Data on waiting times in the Colombian health care system suggest problems. Whilst average waiting time for a consultation with a generalist doctor has fallen from 6.4 days in 2003 to 3.9 days in 2013, delay before seeing a specialist has increased substantially from 10.4 days to 19.2 days over the same period.

Figure 2.2. Average waiting times, days, for a consultation with a generalist doctor, 2003 and 2013, by socio-economic quintile

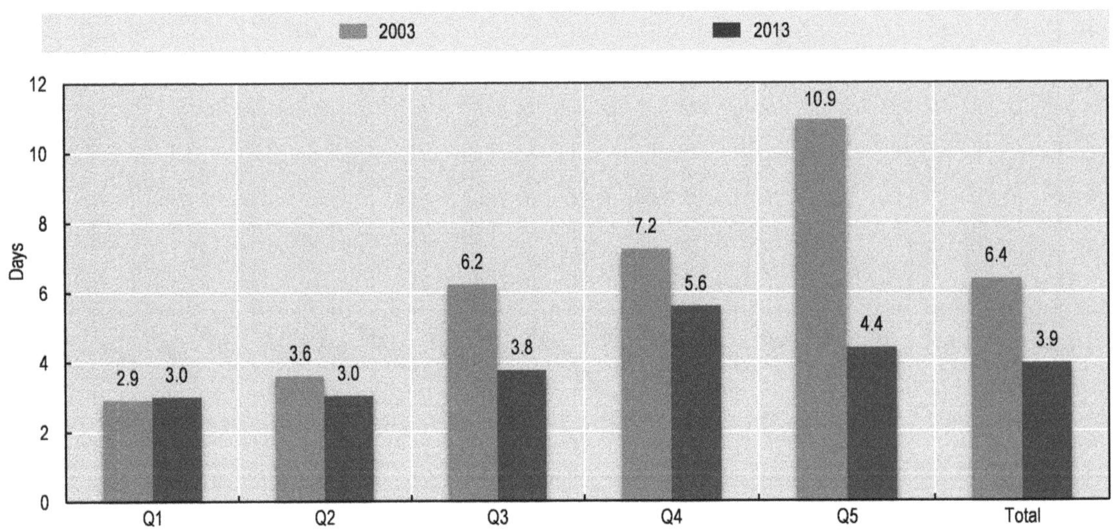

Source: Ministry of Health and Social Protection.

Figure 2.3 shows that waiting times to see a specialist doctor are longer for wealthier income groups. This is consistent with data on the identity of *tutela* litigants, which shows that people from higher socio-economic status tend to be make more frequent use of the litigation mechanism in health care (Bernal et al., 2013). As health conditions are normally poorer in the lower income quintiles and the quality of care received by

SR enrolees seems to be typically lower than in the CR (see below), the greater use of *tutelas* among the better-off further may reflect inequities in access according to socio-economic status.

Figure 2.3. Average waiting times, days, for specialist appointments 2003 and 2013, by socio-economic quintile

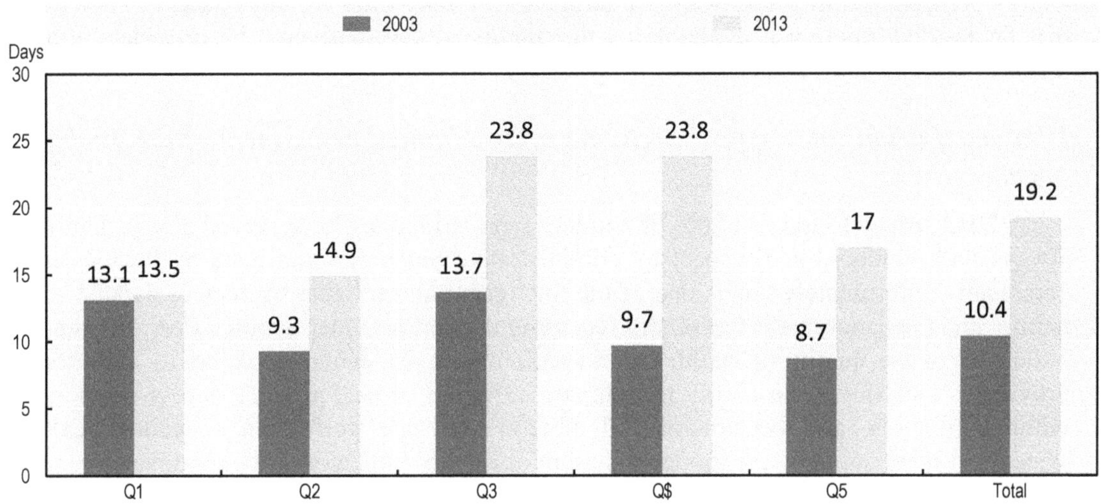

Source: Ministry of Health and Social Protection.

In addition to measures to mitigate the negative consequences of litigation (discussed in the section on cost escalation below), the Colombian Government must keep its commitment to equalise *de facto* the packages offered by the SR and CR as described in Chapter 1, as well as invest in measures to improve the overall quality of services provided. Continuous improvement in the timeliness with which people obtain access to care and in the general quality of care provided would serve as a force to push the litigation trend down.

Regional inequalities continue to be a challenge

Indicators such as maternal and neonatal mortality rates tend to be higher in rural areas and for specific population groups (e.g., indigenous and Roma people). Rural departments such as Guainía, Vichada, Chocó, Amazonas and San Andrés had for example infant mortality rates above 20 per 1 000 live born in 2010. These rates are 71 to 80% higher than the national average of 12.76 deaths per 1 000 live born in 2010 (MSPS, 2013). This suggests that important differences favouring urban areas concerning ease of access to primary and secondary care, which is supported by the higher service utilisation rates in urban areas. There are many potential reasons for this situation. Given the remoteness of many areas in Colombia, factors such as the poor availability of health centres and health professionals, deficient transportation and high transportation costs make it extremely challenging to ensure an adequate standard of care quality in remote locations.

Part of the solution for these issues lies in rearranging the incentive framework (financial and non-financial) for providers and insurers, topics discussed in more depth below in this chapter. Other initiatives may include the development of models of care specific to rural and remote areas. The latter topic is further developed in Chapter 3.

2.3. Quality of health care provision

A system of care quality information and monitoring is in place in Colombia but many operating health institutions still struggle to report valid (or any) data. This means that far less information is available on the quality of care delivered by providers at all levels of complexity than is needed.

User satisfaction rates appear high, but offer a limited assessment of the quality of care

A 2014 survey found that 80% of enrolees reported having been served always/almost always with kindness and respect by administrative personnel and 85% by health care personnel. Unfortunately this is one of the few recent and reliable sources of data on the matter, and the panorama is worse still regarding data on provider quality. Very few other indicators of the quality of health care in Colombia exist, whether nationally or across providers. This limits the ability to compare variation in performance across providers within Colombia, and benchmark Colombia's aggregate performance against health systems in other countries. Although a system of quality indicators is being developed, as described in Chapter 1 (Section 1.6), the majority of these indicators are process rather than outcome measures. Further assessment of this initiative, the *Observatorio de Calidad* (calidadensalud.minsalud.gov.co), can be found in Chapter 3 (Section 3.4).

Some indicators of health care quality are available from other sources, but these are very limited. The CONCORD study of international cancer survival estimates is perhaps the most useful (Allemani, 2015).This finds that five-year survival estimates after a diagnosis of breast, cervical or colorectal cancer are lower in Colombia than the OECD average, but comparable with regional peers such as Chile (Figures 2.4 to 2.6).

Figure 2.4. Breast cancer five-year relative survival rate, 2004-09 (or nearest period)

Age-standardised rates (%)

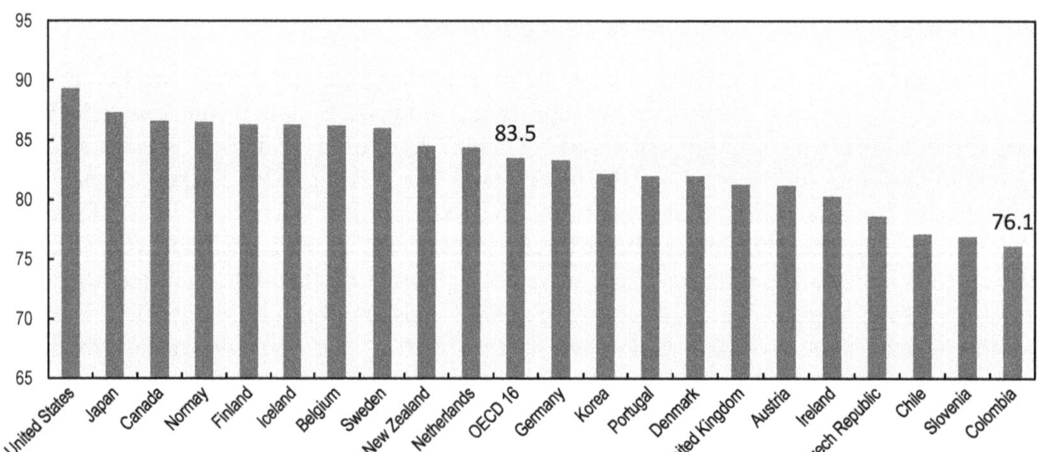

Source: OECD Health Statistics 2015, http://dx.doi.org/10.1787/health-data-en. Data for Colombia and Chile from Allemani, C. et al. (2015), "Global Surveillance of Cancer Survival 1995-2009: Analysis of Individual Data for 25 676 887 Patients from 279 Population-based Registries in 67 Countries (CONCORD-2)", *The Lancet*, Vol. 385, pp. 977-1010, www.thelancet.com/pdfs/journals/lancet/PIIS0140-6736(14)62038-9.pdf.

Figure 2.5. Cervical cancer five-year relative survival rate, 2004-09 (or nearest period)

Age-standardised rates (%)

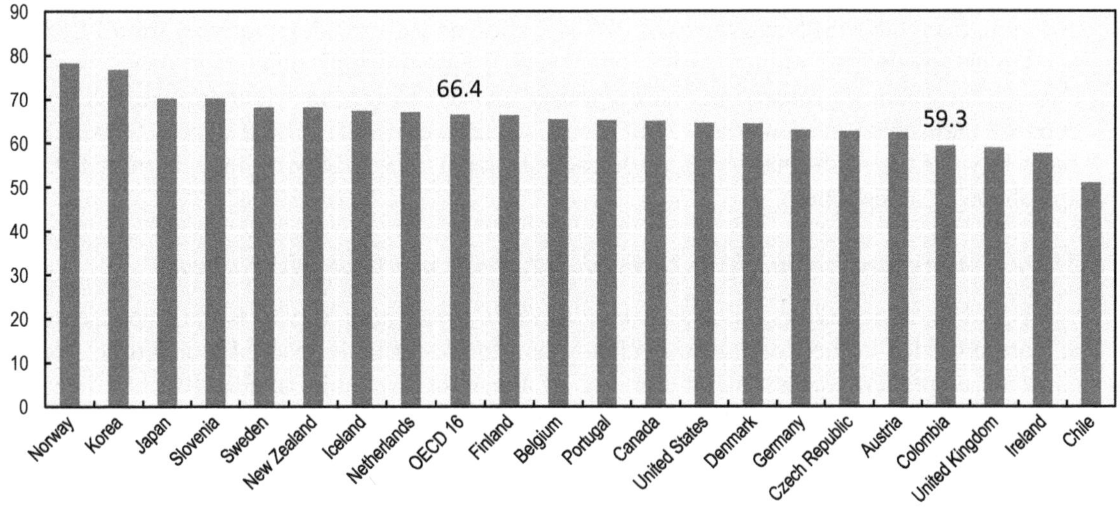

Source: OECD Health Statistics 2015, http://dx.doi.org/10.1787/health-data-en. Data for Colombia and Chile from Allemani, C. et al. (2015), "Global Surveillance of Cancer Survival 1995-2009: Analysis of Individual Data for 25 676 887 Patients from 279 Population-based Registries in 67 Countries (CONCORD-2)", *The Lancet*, Vol. 385, pp. 977-1010, www.thelancet.com/pdfs/journals/lancet/PIIS0140-6736(14)62038-9.pdf.

Figure 2.6. Colorectal cancer five-year relative survival rate by sex, 2004-09 (or nearest period)

Age-standardised rates (%)

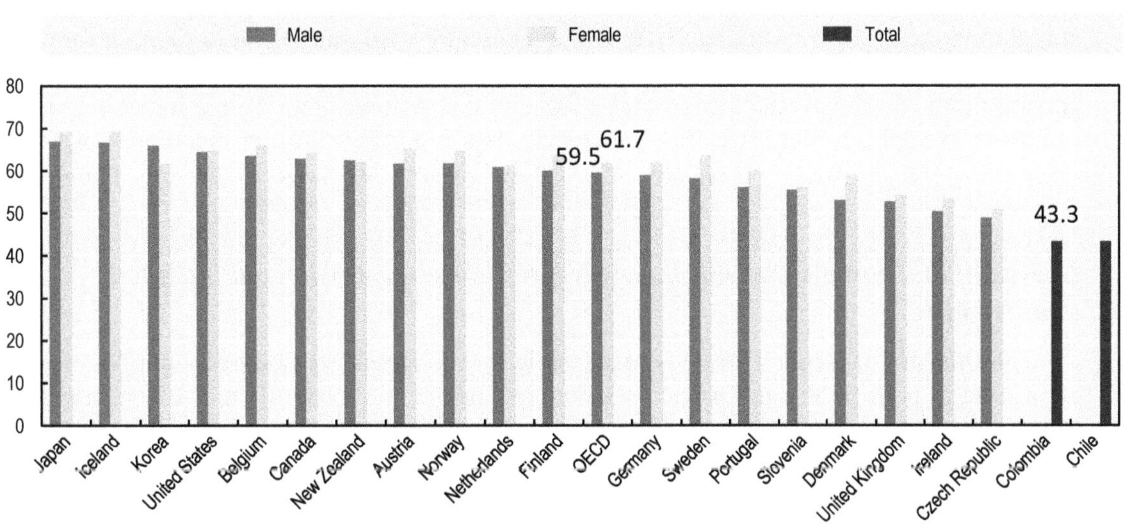

Source: OECD Health Statistics 2015, http://dx.doi.org/10.1787/health-data-en. Data for Colombia and Chile from Allemani, C. et al. (2015), "Global Surveillance of Cancer Survival 1995-2009: Analysis of Individual Data for 25 676 887 Patients from 279 Population-based Registries in 67 Countries (CONCORD-2)", *The Lancet*, Vol. 385, pp. 977-1010, www.thelancet.com/pdfs/journals/lancet/PIIS0140-6736(14)62038-9.pdf.

The scarcity of reliable quality data is an issue that must be addressed with urgency by Colombian authorities, as much of the performance of a managed competition model hinges on the public availability of quality data to support user choice of insurer and provider and spur quality-driven competition.

For the EPS of both regimes there have been surveys conducted by the MSPS to evaluate user-satisfaction with services, ranking EPS according to performance. These rankings have been published in individual reports for each EPS (*carta de desempeño*) available from the MSPS and the own EPS websites, as well as comparatively for all EPS in tables available online from the health monitoring and oversight body (*Superintendencia de Salud*). EPS are required by law to provide new enrolees with a copy of their *carta de desempeño*, but there is scarce evidence on the degree to which users rely on such information to guide their decisions about leaving their current EPS and choosing a new one.

More comprehensive quality information systems are being developed

SISPRO (*Sistema Integral de Información de la Protección Social*) is the database on all care provided in the Colombian health system to the formally insured population. The current comprehensiveness and reliability of the data available at SISPRO has been questioned. This is a crucial impediment for users to make informed choices of insurer and provider based on the standard of services offered as envisaged when the health reforms of the early 1990s were introduced. For example, comparable data on many clinical indicators in primary care and inpatient care (e.g. infection rates, waiting times) is virtually inexistent at the system level. In specific areas, such as cancer care, there is a strong need for the collection of more detailed data on basic aspects of process and outcomes like survival rates, which are virtually non-existent even in the leading national institutions.

For mechanisms such as free choice of insurer to have a decisive effect on levels of system efficiency and quality, it is imperative also that good information on the performance of providers is collected and made available to users in a widely, timely and straightforward fashion. Although SISPRO is gradually evolving into a usable platform for information on provider indicators, there seems to be little knowledge among the general public on the availability of that information and how such information could be used, for example, to compare IPS. Moreover, data reporting is often incomplete with respect to both the range of system actors included and the scope of the information provided.

Oversight and competition mechanisms have not always delivered intended quality gains

The Ministry of Health (MoH) is responsible for the regulatory and oversight policies applicable to both public and private institutions and for all levels of care. Licensing is the minimum requirement for a health care provider to operate in Colombia, with clinical and operational standards defined and assessed by the MSPS. An accreditation process has been introduced to encourage providers to adopt quality standards above the minimum requirements. Accreditation is voluntary for providers, but the incentives for adoption are weak, largely due to the lack of actual user choice of provider based on quality indicators. Currently, only 31 hospitals (IPS) have been awarded accreditation in Colombia, corresponding to less than 0.3% of the total number of IPS. The positive influence of the accreditation system on overall care quality levels is therefore probably negligible at this point.

This situation is compounded by a trend for vertical integration between insurers and providers. Vertical integration was permitted in the 1990s reforms and is currently limited by law to a 30% of the total health related spending by the EPS. Nonetheless, regulatory loopholes that allow, for example, insurers to essentially impose contracts with exclusivity clauses hamper the potential for actual market competition for patients. In this context vertical integration also acts as an entry barrier to competitors in the insurance market, tying up scarce services – for example, the only hospital operating in an area – to incumbent insurers, hence making these services unavailable to potential entrants who seek to establish contracts with the same provider (Zweifel, 2011). This situation further curtails the potential efficiency and quality gains from the Colombian health reforms.

The model of managed competition between insurers can only bring about system efficiency and quality gains if genuine, informed user choice exists alongside a carefully designed and binding regulatory framework. This is clear from the experience of other countries where broadly similar models of purchaser-provider split have been developed. In contrast to the prevailing situation in countries like the Netherlands however, topics such as vertical integration between insurers and providers and the quality assurance framework remain unresolved regulatory issues in Colombia.

2.4. Financial sustainability

As detailed in Chapter 1, health funds in Colombia come from a variety of mandatory sources. These are mainly employee and employer payroll contributions for the CR, and public sources (national and local tax revenues) and cross-subsidisation from CR funds in the case of SR. FOSYGA (*Fondo de Solidaridad y Garantia*) is the institution in charge of pooling health funds accruing to the CR, whereas funds for the SR are pooled at the national and (mainly) local levels. Insurer institutions (*Entidades Prestadoras de Servicios*, EPS) receive their revenues through a capitated payment (UPC) per enrolee, with some adjustment for geographic, demographic and – to a lesser extent – epidemiologic factors in the case of CR enrolees, while a flat UPC has applied in practice to reimburse care provided to SR enrolees.

Figure 2.7. Total health expenditure as a share of GDP in Colombia and OECD countries, 2013

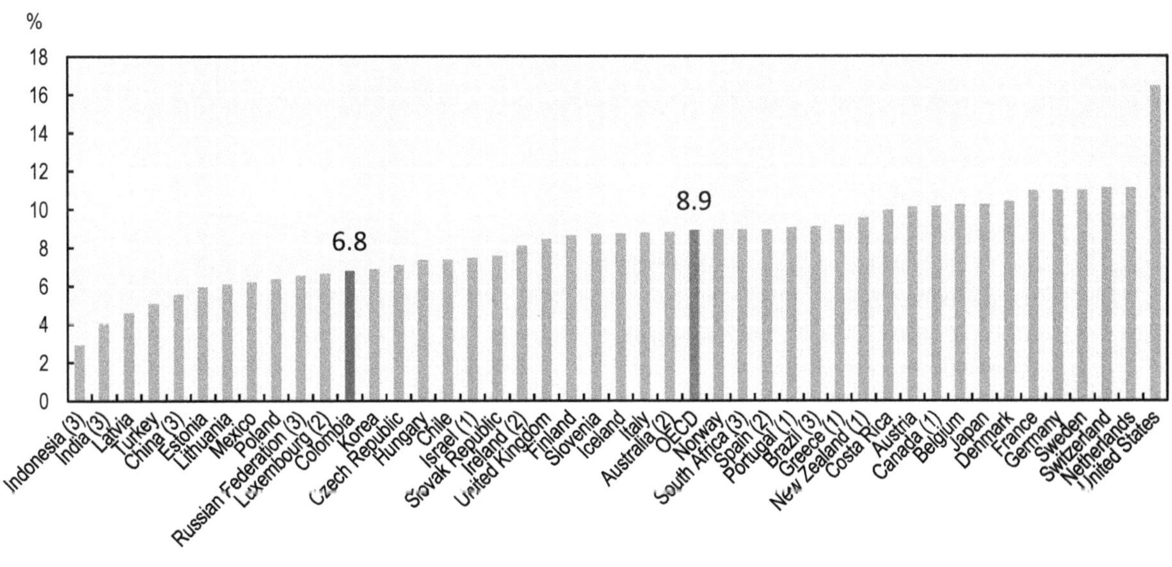

1. Preliminary estimates. 2. Data refers to 2012. 3. Total health expenditure (including capital expenditure).

Source: OECD Health Statistics 2015, http://dx.doi.org/ 10.1787/health-data-en and WHO Global Health Expenditure Database, http://apps.who.int/nha/database.

Signs of upward pressure on health care spending are apparent

Overall, levels of health funding in Colombia were somewhat lower than those from most OECD countries in 2012 (Figure 2.7). The most recent figures for Colombia point to spending of around 7% of national GDP in the health sector. More than three-quarters of that spending come from public sources, a figure above the OECD average (Figure 2.8); this share has been on the rise recently and the government sees the possibility of further increases in the coming years.

Figure 2.8. Government health expenditure in Colombia and OECD countries, 2012

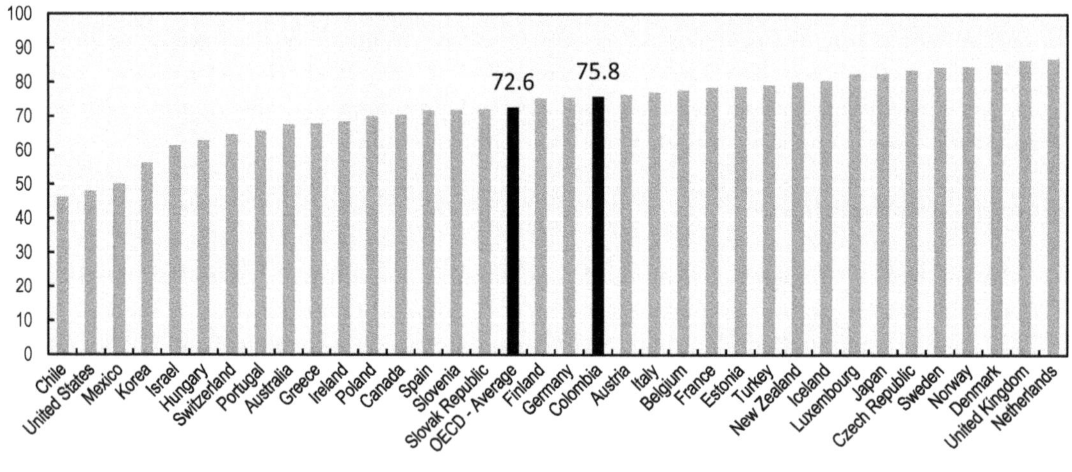

Source: OECD Health Statistics 2015, http://dx.doi.org/ 10.1787/health-data-en.

Health care spending in absolute levels has been climbing steeply in recent years, particularly in the SR. As a share of GDP, however, spending has remained more or less constant, running between 6.5% and 6.8% between 2010 and 2013 (Figure 2.9).

Figure 2.9. Health spending growth in COP and as a percentage of GDP

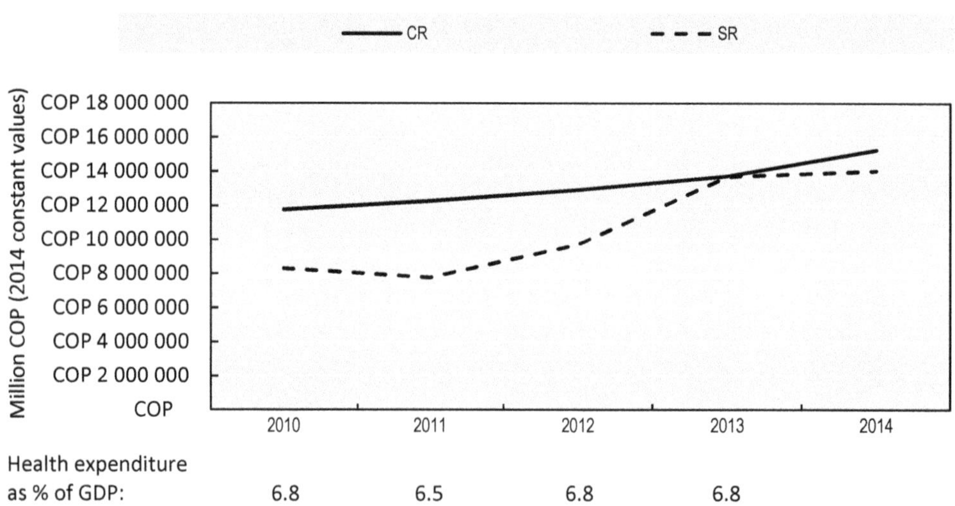

CR: Contributory regime; SR: Subsidised regime.

Source: Ministry of Health and Social Protection and *OECD Health Statistics 2015*, http://dx.doi.org/10.1787/health-data-en.

In addition to freeing up extra resources through efficiency improvements within the health sector (discussed below in Section 2.6), further increases contemplated by the government in the absolute and relative amount of resources going into the health sector are likely to be vital for the financial sustainability of the system and care quality levels in the coming years. The UPC has been continuously adjusted upwards in the last ten years for both the SR and CR, with forecasted increments of between 8.5% and 11% for the year 2016, and 10% for 2017 (Dávila, 2015). These continuous upwards adjustments to the UPC – usually at levels above inflation – will be necessary to guarantee that the equalisation of the SR benefit package to the benefit package offered to CR members that as mandated in 2012, both in terms of the range of services and the quality of their provision.

The UPC received per enrolee at each age band seems to track average costs relatively well for most age categories except for the over 70s, whereupon a flat UPC falls consistently below average costs (Bolivar, 2014). The available data suggests some potential for cross-subsidisation (possibly at a gain) of the cost of services for older populations from surpluses obtained in the provision of services for the younger individuals, which may help explain the relatively large number of EPS (17 in the CR, 35 in the SR; PROESA, 2015) still operating in the Colombian market more than 20 years after the enactment of Law 100.

Some factors raise concerns about the sustainability of the multiple insurer model. EPS are too often acting as mere financial clearing-houses, lacking effective engagement with either consumers or providers. Financial supervision has been weak, leading to well-publicised cases of misuse of funds by EPS. The number of EPS has been falling as of 2004 with cases of insurers ceasing to operate due to financial difficulties. It may be of course that some of these EPS have been driven away from the market due to inefficiencies and generally poor performance in a competitive environment. Yet the fact that the EPS within the CR as a group reported net financial losses in 2013 and 2014 suggests a systemic problem (Table 2.1). These financial losses for EPS within the CR are even larger if the accounting exercise excludes those revenues yet to be received for services provided via the mechanism of *tutelas* (see below), which are reimbursed retrospectively by FOSYGA on a fee-for-service basis, but that are often not reimbursed in full.

Table 2.1. Consolidated net financial results of EPS within the contributory and subsidised regimes

	Million COP		Million USD	
EPS group	September 2013	September 2014	September 2013	September 2014
Contributory regime	-638 260	-192 473	-220	-66
Subsidised regime	2 627 248	7 710	907	3

Source: "Cuestión Salud", No. 08, Year 3, February. Available at: http://www.proesa.org.co. (accessed April 2015).

Although the situation is somewhat less acute for the EPS within the SR, which reported small net financial gains in 2014, such gains have been dwindling consistently in recent years due both to increases in total expenditures and reductions in revenues (+23% and -22% between 2013-14, respectively; PROESA, 2015). The rise in spending is likely to reflect in no small part the expansions in the number of people covered by the SR, the equalisation of the benefit package offered to SR enrolees to that offered to CR members, and a consequent rise in service use within the SR. Despite an important increase since 2011 in the UPC applicable to insurers within the SR, such increase in real terms does not seem to have been sufficient to counterbalance the substantial and continued growth in expenditures per enrolee (Núñez et al., 2012).

Financial challenges are apparent as well from the perspective of providers (*Instituciones Prestadoras de Servicios de Salud*, IPS). In the public sector – where there is more information available on financial indicators – the operational deficit of hospitals reached about USD 62 million in 2012. The generally poor financial health of public hospitals has been attributed to two main groups of factors. The first reason has been some delays by the EPS in the payment of services provided and complete default on payments owed by those EPS that have ceased operations. The second group of factors refers to poor operational efficiency and financial management of resources by hospitals in a scenario of expanding insurance coverage and higher demand for services, compounded by a reduction in direct payments made by the smaller uninsured population (Uribe, 2009). A recent study investigating the levels of productivity in public hospitals has found evidence of generalised resource constraints reflected in scarce investments in new technologies, with damaging consequences for productivity levels (Orozco Gallo, 2014). An assessment of the financial conditions of 968 public hospitals concluded that as many as 45% of these institutions were at high risk of financial breakdown in 2014 – compared to 32% in 2012 (Superintendencia Nacional de Salud, 2013). In many cases hospital closures have been avoided by financial rescue operations by the national and local governments, despite a high profile case of hospital closure in Barranquilla in 2008.

Although some of the reasons for the financial challenges faced by EPS and IPS refer primarily to efficiency aspects, other challenges discussed above arise from an interrupted or insufficient flow of revenues, as in the case of institutions operating in catchment areas with relatively more deprived or older populations. Plans to risk adjust the UPC and transfer of resources are being developed. These are further discussed in Section 2.6.

High rates of informality present a challenge to sustainable revenue raising

The Colombian Government is aware of the need to increase resource allocations to the health sector to formally equalise the benefit packages of the subsidised and contributory regimes, both in terms of coverage and quality. Plans have been developed to introduce so-called "sin" taxes earmarked for health on the consumption of sugared soft drinks, following the example of Mexico and other countries in the OECD. The intention announced by the government is to impose a flat levy per sugared drink consumed. Additional resources raised will be directed specifically to the financing of public health programmes (targeted at conditions such as obesity and diabetes), as well as investments in hospital infrastructure. These extra funds should enlarge the pool of resources available in the health sector, and add to new revenues being raised by local governments with the same purpose. One example of the latter is the use by the Barranquilla district of revenues raised through stamp duty to fund investments in health infrastructure.

A key challenge to keep raising revenues for the health sector is the general issue of informality in the economy. Around half of the total health system funding comes from contributory sources (payroll contributions) and it has proven difficult to increase this component of funding due to the important magnitude of the informal labour market. Recent studies estimate that informal employment accounts for between 50% and 70% of total employment in Colombia depending on the particular definition of informality, one of the highest rates in Latin America (OECD, 2015). This situation reduces the contributory and tax bases posing obvious financing hurdles to all public sectors, exacerbated in the health sector in light of an ageing population and expansions in the range of services included in the publicly-funded package.

Recently, the Colombian Government has attempted to tackle some of the constraints imposed on revenue raising by labour market informality (as well as perceived widespread tax evasion) by moving away from contributory sources in the health sector. In 2013, employer contributions were in practice replaced by a new tax over net annual profits (*Contribución Empresarial para la Equidad*, CREE), a surtax of 9% on corporate income. The CREE surtax is planned to increase to 18% during the period 2015-18, replacing a wealth tax on companies (OECD, 2015). Even though the introduction of CREE has contributed to a rise in income taxes as share of GDP (to 6.8% in 2013 from 5.5% in the previous year; OECD, 2015), its effects on health sector budgets are unclear as CREE revenues are directed to the "social sector" as a whole, not just health. Since the new tax has different reporting and collection mechanisms compared to other levies such as income tax, it is unclear how far it can reduce the problem of tax evasion and the consequent reduction of resources for health.

Cost escalation and the judicialisation of health care are also threats to sustainability

An analysis of the expenditures per enrolee indicates that these have been increasing substantially in both regimes, essentially due to a higher number of services provided per user (Núñez et al., 2012). Total expenditure in laboratory tests was the spending category with the highest growth among EPS between 2006 and 2008 (31%). Alongside medical consultations, laboratory tests represent around half of the services provided by EPS, and the major cost growth driver in both cases has been the rising number of services provided (growth rates of around 45% and 25% for the number of tests and consultations provided, respectively, compared to unit price reductions of around 10% in both cases).

As mentioned before, part of the increased demand for these services may reflect broader access to the system by populations with previously unmet needs, particularly among SR enrolees benefitting from a wider package of services covered. It may also reflect efficiency gains achieved by EPS now able to charge reduced prices for same quality services. But the fact that the rise in service utilisation has happened to a degree far higher than unit price changes, coupled with slow improvements in health outcomes in Colombia during the last decade (see Section 2.5), has led to speculation about the role played by EPS in inducing demand for service, perhaps as a way to compensate for perceived discrepancies between the actual costs for certain groups of patients and the corresponding UPC received.

There is also another important dimension to the issue of demand pressures on costs in the Colombian health system. As mentioned in Section 2.2. The intense judicialisation of health care resource allocation decisions in the country reflects general systemic failures. Deficiencies in the provision of timely and quality services included in the POS spur legal challenges particularly among better informed populations. Between November 2011 and November 2012, 75% of *tutelas* referred to delays in the provision of services, and 42% of the total number of *tutelas* referred to services included in the basic benefit package (Bernal et al., 2013).

Data for the period 2002-05 indicate that total expenditures by the EPS referring to services provided under *tutelas* and presented to FOSYGA for reimbursement have been on the rise. This phenomenon is likely to have contributed to the weak financial position of many EPS as seen above, as reimbursement by FOSYGA has often been only partial for services not included in the basic package. In the CR, spending on these services represents around a quarter of the total and grew by a factor of 120 between 2002 and 2010 (Núñez et al., 2012). Deleterious consequences arise also for national and sub-national governments, since the funds to reimburse service provision excluded from POS but granted by *tutelas* must in the end be met by FOSYGA (in the CR case) or local departments (in the SR), and come from sources other than the contributions and taxes introduced specifically to finance health care.

In spite of the above, there are still incentives in the system for some insurers and providers to encourage individuals to request new and costly therapies through *tutelas*. EPS may see the resources from *tutelas* reimbursed by the government as another partial compensation for UPC below actual costs for certain patients. The stronger incentive to promote *tutelas* may lie in the pharmaceutical area. This is illustrated by the fact that the reimbursement of *tutelas* referring to drugs excluded from POS grew by a factor of 19 000 (reaching COP 1 billion, USD 345 000 or EUR 314 000) from 2001 to 2008 (Núñez et al., 2012). This explosive situation was probably spurred by a complete lack of regulation by Colombian authorities of the price of medicines excluded from POS until very recently, in contrast to regulated prices for pharmaceuticals included in POS. The national government has taken steps to regain control over such expenditures, mainly by imposing ceilings on the reimbursement of the most common drugs requested through *tutelas* in 2011, but also by including some of these drugs in POS with maximum reimbursement prices (see Box 1.4).

2.5. Efficiency aspects

The public-private mix and decentralised nature of the Colombian health system make the co-ordination and stewardship tasks by the MSPS all the more important – and yet all the more difficult. In particular, the MSPS should take a more active role in the co-ordination of human resource and infrastructure investments by operating institutions in order to raise efficiency standards. The MSPS should also seek to gradually (but decisively) address weaknesses of the current framework of financial and non-financial incentives facing providers and insurers, so as to encourage efficiency and quality gains in the system.

The distribution and reimbursement of human resources is not as efficient as it could be

Although data on the availability of doctors per capita show similar numbers to other countries of the region (14 doctors per 10 000 people), these are below the figures for most OECD countries, and the figures are even lower for nurse professionals (see Chapter 1). There is a well-documented scarcity of general doctors particularly outside urban localities; in remote or small municipalities the typical number of doctors per 10 000 people is around or usually below one. The relatively low number of general doctors in most Colombian municipalities may be in part a result of weak incentives to pursue such a career among medicine graduates, as discussed in Chapter 3.

The situation does not improve much as far as the availability of specialist doctors is concerned. The rapid growth in insurance affiliation in recent years has resulted in an increase in demand for specialist services which has been higher than the corresponding growth in the supply of specialist doctors. A study commissioned by the MSPS in 2013 included a survey of IPS managers and found that more than 55% of these managers considered their group of specialists to be incomplete, with more than half of the managers having reported the scrapping of at least one service in the previous five years due to unavailability of doctors in the corresponding speciality (Amaya Lara et al., 2013). Particular areas of concern are Internal Medicine, Paediatrics, Gynaecology and Obstetrics, General Surgery and Psychiatry, among others. As in the case of general doctors, the location of specialists tends to be heavily concentrated – four departments (Bogotá, Antioquia, Valle del Cauca and Atlántico, representing 44% of the country's population) account for 72% of the total number of specialists.

In addition to imbalances in the supply of health professionals, system efficiency and quality are hampered by the current allocation of financial resources and the framework of financial incentives faced by the health workforce. Administrative costs represent a sizeable burden to (public and private) providers and insurers. According to the results of one study focused on public providers, the ratio of medical care-related staff per administrative staff reached 0.57 on average, well below an often cited international standard of three medical care per administrative staff (Sarmiento Gómez et al., 2005). Expenditures with administrative personnel were estimated to represent on average 25.8% of the total payroll in that group of providers. Factors such as the growth in *tutelas* and the associated bureaucratic and legal processes EPS need to go through in order to obtain reimbursement from FOSYGA, as well as the coexistence of various different reimbursement procedures and information systems used by EPS, FOSYGA and the MSPS, have been advanced as likely drivers of administrative costs and potential allocative inefficiencies in the system.

From the point of view of the financial incentive framework, the system of incentives embedded into payment mechanisms for health professionals has remained basically untouched in the 1993 reforms. This system provides weak stimulus to continuous quality improvements in the provision of care, since most professionals are paid solely through fixed salaries (with no link to performance assessment), and in many instances contracts are temporary and do not include social security benefits. Evidence from other national settings have concluded that movements away from salary mechanisms for health professionals are a successful strategy to raise allocative efficiency, for example through the strengthening of the primary care system, by improving user experience (when remuneration is at least partly tied to performance) as well as prevention of more expensive care, including avoidable hospitalisations (Moreno-Serra, 2014).

Similar concerns apply to the institutions providing health care

The main challenge concerning physical health resources in Colombia pertains to their distribution. Providers tend to be largely concentrated in densely populated areas, with a notable increase in the number of private providers in those localities in the last ten years. In contrast, populations living in remote and rural provinces such as Chocó have very little choice of provider even for simple outpatient care. Providers in these areas tend to be public and often struggle with issues such as high operational costs and difficulties to attract and maintain health professionals, which is likely to affect the quality of care provided.

The MSPS has limited control over infrastructure investment decisions made by the private sector, but could do more to reframe incentives to the latter and – particularly – to induce quality improvements in public provision. As detailed below, this involves stronger leadership by the MSPS on infrastructure planning, perhaps including financial and non-financial incentives for private providers to enter areas currently dominated by the public sector. It should also include revised financial incentives to public providers through the introduction of prospective, patient-based reimbursement mechanisms (virtually inexistent nowadays). It is important that the move towards activity-based reimbursement encompasses elements of selective contracting that ensure the presence of primary care providers in remote areas, as well as (easy access to) higher level providers, through for instance funding tied specifically to the provision of a list of services considered as a priority in these localities.

Robust assessment of health system performance is hampered in Colombia by poor information systems

Recent econometric studies have shown the substantial population health benefits obtained by countries that increase reliance on pooled funds in the total financing of the health system (Moreno-Serra and Smith, 2012). Case studies in specific countries have also highlighted important gains in terms of access to care and financial protection due to expansions in formal health insurance coverage (Lagomarsino et al., 2012). However, there are no robust published analyses quantifying the health gains from the reforms introduced in Colombia since 1993. There is some perception that health outcomes have been improving at a slower rate than desired, but there is little quantitative information to support these claims, specifically with regard to the health system contributions to these trends. More evidence on this, as well as on the impacts of specific aspects of the reforms – for example the extent of actual competition between insurers for users – is needed.

It is possible that some of the slow progress in health outcomes vis-à-vis the growth in spending is due to constraints in the health system's information infrastructure. Insurers and providers in the private sector maintain their own information systems on financial and clinical aspects, and even though there are legal requirements for private actors to submit key financial data (e.g. investments) to the MSPS, it has been reported that the number of providers submitting information is much smaller than the group of providers not reporting any data whatsoever (Núñez et al., 2012). One of the negative consequences of this incomplete reporting and absence of a single system of national health accounts is hampering the MSPS capacity to co-ordinate investments on new infrastructure according to local needs, which may result in sub-optimal care provision and population health outcomes.

2.6. Priorities for improving health system performance

Increased focus on primary care access and adequate integration with other levels of care should be Colombia's foremost priority

The fact that primary, secondary and tertiary care are provided by public and private institutions according to SR and CR affiliation, creates obstacles for an adequate integration of provision and continuity of care. Some of these obstacles have started being addressed by the incipient development of differential models of care in rural and remote areas as mentioned above, whose expansion must continue to be supported by the MSPS.

In particular, regional models based on community health teams (as seen in Barranquilla and some neighbouring cities) look promising and should be encouraged through initiatives including technical assistance and good practice dissemination. Such regional models, if tailored adequately according to local epidemiologic and resource challenges, can promote system efficiency by reducing costs at higher levels of care by expanding access to health prevention and promotion activities. This result has been seen in Barranquilla, where the implementation of the locally developed model of health teams has been accompanied by a reduction in the utilisation of high-cost services (Núñez et al., 2012).

Box 2.1. Barranquilla's model of health service delivery

Barranquilla has achieved 100% enrolment in health insurance for its 1.2m population, with just over half enrolled in the SR. The city equalised entitlements and services across the CR and SR regimes in 2008, a few years ahead of the Constitutional Court ruling that required equalisation across the health system. This, as well as infrastructure investment in the physical infrastructure of Barranquilla's health services, was partly financed by a ring-fenced tax on households (equivalent to 0.5% of buildings value).

The city has developed a distinctive model of providing health care services, with an emphasis on integrated care and primary and preventive care. A single IPS provides all local health services, which comprise a network of one rehabilitation centre, nine hospitals (of which eight are smaller units, offering women and children's services only) and 33 primary care centres. All citizens are within one kilometre of one of these centres, which are seen as the basis of the wider health care system and offer an integrated, multidisciplinary approach to prevention and primary care. A notable feature of this approach is Barranquilla's team of *caminantes* ("walkers"). These are health promotion specialists, each of whom works directly with ~200 assigned households. *Caminantes* assess personal and household health risks, advise on health promotion and monitor individuals with long-term health care needs. Each is equipped with a tablet computer, so that public health data can be stored and analysed electronically.

The city can point to a number of successes. 96% of local residents report being satisfied with local services. Emergency hospital attendances fell by 16% between 2012 and 2014 60% of adults aged between 18 and 69 report daily physical activity. Persistent challenges include high rates of teenage pregnancy, for which the municipality has launched an intersectoral initiative involving both health and school services.

In order to allow local models to spread and succeed in expanding effective access to care and raising efficiency, it is crucial that the MSPS makes renewed efforts to clarify the responsibilities of *entidades territoriales* (ET, or local governments) vis-à-vis national authorities. Following the example of other OECD countries, ET responsibility might focus on primary care and community care facilities, and the local models could be developed around these areas. Additional responsibilities for ET may include some quality assurance, monitoring and improvement of local (particularly public) IPS. Yet assurance and monitoring activities in many health systems are primarily performed at higher administrative levels – often independent bodies at arms' length from the MSPS (as the Care Quality Commission in England) – also to benefit from economies of scale in such activities. Thus any transferring of assurance and monitoring roles to ET must be accompanied by MSPS support in terms of additional resources and training to fulfil these roles.

Furthermore, the MSPS needs to play a more active role in mitigating potential market failures in the Colombian primary care market. In an environment where insurers compete for patients there may be strong incentives for insurers to reduce resources dedicated to prevention and promotion activities (van de Ven and Schut, 2011). This is because patients of a given insurer may benefit from such activities only to migrate to another insurer after some time, where the latter company will reap the rewards of healthier enrolees in the future without having incurred the associated costs. A more demanding performance framework for ET needs to be developed by the MSPS, focussed on preventive care (but including broader aspects of care) and population health outcomes.

A more strategic approach to infrastructure planning and use of the private sector to meet local health care needs is vital, including financial and non-financial incentives for private providers to enter areas currently monopolised by the public sector or areas with virtually no health care facilities. In remote areas, however, IPS monopolies of provision may be a way to improve the financial sustainability of providers dealing with sicker populations, as well as favour the development of integrated care pathways by ensuring the presence of at least one accessible provider for each level of care – an important challenge for some ET. This should be assessed on a case-by-case basis and, should a monopolist IPS be allowed to operate in a given area, it should be closely monitored according to assurance and monitoring procedures as mentioned previously, held jointly accountable with the ET for results in terms of population health outcomes. The issue of financial and non-financial incentives to payers and providers to spur quality gains in the Colombian system is further developed in the section on incentives below.

Promotion of real patient choice as a tool to improve quality should also be prioritised

The MSPS has a crucial role to play in enabling actual patient choice of insurer and provider. Regulatory measures to address the issues of vertical integration and lack of incentives for provider accreditation should be top of the agenda. The experience of other countries that have established a purchaser-provider split with purchaser competition can be helpful in this respect, as discussed below.

In more densely populated areas where insurer competition is feasible, it would seem appropriate to discourage vertical integration of payers and providers by strongly enforcing current limits (30% of a given EPS total health related spending) and perhaps setting an even lower threshold. In the Netherlands, the pro-market reforms rolled out during the 1990s, which included the move towards purchaser and provider competition, as well as allowing health funds not to contract with all individual providers, have seen very limited vertical integration between insurers and providers (Schut and van de Ven, 2011). Until recently, only one major purchaser had vertically integrated with providers. This situation has arisen mainly due to a political consensus around the undesirability of growing vertical integration in the Dutch context. Proposals that could expand current levels of vertical integration – for instance, the proposed set up of a co-operative in 2008 involving a regional health insurer, a regional physician co-operative and other health professionals, in order to take over a local hospital in financial distress – have been strongly opposed in Parliament, based on concerns about professional autonomy and free choice of provider by users.

The Dutch experience provides a good illustration for the Colombian health system of how purchaser competition is capable of succeeding as a strategy to improve efficiency and quality. Insurers are free to compete for enrolees through adjustments to their community-rated premiums and this has resulted in strong price competition among insurers. Stronger competition for enrolees through policy prices quickly translated into financial pressure on insurers, whose general reaction has been two-fold (Schut and Van de Ven, 2011). First, there has been wider experimentation and adoption of measures to reduce operational and managerial costs. Increased participation in health promotion activities and development of disease management programmes for chronic conditions have also been observed as strategies to reduce future treatment costs. Second, insurers have been more active in pushing for lower prices when contracting with individual providers, an outcome facilitated by the low level of vertical integration. The cost-containment measures adopted by Dutch health insurers do not seem to have had negative effects in terms of the quality of care provided. Average waiting times have fallen significantly owing to the adoption of mechanisms to reduce waiting lists, including mediation services for patients to search for alternative hospitals with shorter waits.

The availability of more and better information for patients on provider and insurer performance has been another driver of quality enhancement efforts in OECD countries, and should be emulated by Colombia. In the Netherlands, a national system to measure consumer experience with health insurers and providers was implemented in 2006 (Shekelle, 2009). This information system publishes widely disseminated consumer scores for health insurers and has consistently shown higher levels of consumer satisfaction in the competitive Dutch system, both in terms of clinical outcomes and processes.

Improvements in the quality of care have also been found after competition between hospitals was stimulated in the English National Health System in the 2000s (Gaynor et al., 2013). General practitioners – who are gatekeepers for referrals to secondary and tertiary care – were required to offer users a choice of provider for elective hospital care under a system known as "Choose and Book". The hospital was then to be chosen by the patient, with the assistance of a doctor, through an electronic system that was purposely developed containing data on indicators such as hospital cleanliness, waiting times, infection and risk-adjusted mortality rates. The English pro-competition reforms encouraged quality-based competition and ultimately patient outcomes, as measured by avoidable mortality indicators (Gaynor et al., 2013). Importantly, quality-based competition between providers was made possible because the "Choose and Book" system was accompanied by a prospective payment mechanism for hospitals through fixed, case mix-adjusted prices. Prospective reimbursement forced providers to compete more intensely in a context where money follows the patient. In the Netherlands, some commentators have noted that the efficiency gains from the Dutch reforms could probably have been larger if health insurers did not have most deficits on hospital expenses frequently reimbursed retrospectively (Schut and Van de Ven, 2011). Alternatives for improving the system of financial incentives for providers in Colombia, as well as to enhance the current information system structure, are further discussed in the sub-sections below.

In addition to a stronger stance on limits to vertical integration between EPS and providers, Colombian authorities should act directly on other measures capable of creating incentives for quality-based competition. These include a more active role by the MSPS in collecting and publicising information on insurer and provider quality indicators to users. From the insurer perspective, EPS performance ratings should be developed and published to encourage innovation, quality and efficiency. Some degree of mergers and acquisitions may be allowed in the EPS market, enabling better-performing and financially sounder EPS to absorb weaker ones, but with a transparent and carefully designed regulatory mechanism in place (as in other areas in the private sector) to mitigate market concentration concerns.

For providers, the MSPS should expand efforts to compile and publicise information on various aspects of care – including outcomes and user satisfaction – and for different levels of care, making such information available to users in a timely and easy manner, following the country experiences described above. Transparent information on the quality of local primary care and community care providers should be one of the priorities, as discussed in Chapter 3. Wide dissemination of provider quality data among users is likely to strengthen the perceived benefits of voluntary accreditation for providers and incentivise its adoption as a signalling mechanism for patient choice (and as a signal also for purchasers within a selective contracting setting; see section on incentives below). At the same time, the regulatory capacity of the *Superintendencia Nacional de*

Salud should be strengthened so that swift and effective action can be taken against poor performers, including in the limit a credible threat of provider closure.

Increased reliance on non-contributory sources of funding will be vital to underpin the health system's financial sustainability

The planned increase in resources aimed to the Colombian health sector in future years, crucial to enabling continued coverage expansions and care quality improvements, should come mainly from pooled financing sources. Several studies have shown that high reliance on out-of-pocket payments – including cost-sharing – in health financing is associated with a higher risk of households being affected by financial catastrophe or being pushed (further) into poverty due to health care payments, or simply foregoing needed treatment due to inability to pay (Moreno-Serra and Smith, 2012). Countries that have been successful in ensuring access to quality care to the vast majority of their populations have done so invariably through insurance mechanisms relying on mandatory, pooled funds coming from taxation and social contributions. This is the case among others in most European countries, Malaysia, South Korea, and more recently in Costa Rica and Thailand.

Colombia has acknowledged the importance of relying on pooled financing to achieve universal coverage since the inception of the health reforms in the 1990s. Given the already high burden of contributory levies on employers and employees (even compared to other Latin American countries; OECD, 2015), further health revenue growth will be more feasible if based on general taxation sources, whose increased stability compared to contributory funds is also likely to contribute positively to the system's long term financial sustainability. The Colombian Government needs to keep shifting the focus towards general taxes as the main basis of health care financing and should maintain its commitment to transfer more revenues to the health sector, as demonstrated by the impending introduction of earmarked "sin" taxes, while limiting user co-payments as a financing source.

Should the increase in the CREE surtax between 2015 and 2018 take place as planned by the authorities, it is important that an adequate share of this is allocated to the health sector. Although not directly under the control of the MSPS, it would be advisable to push for some earmarking of CREE revenues to health, as this could serve as a way of further protecting spending in the health sector when finances are tight, and facilitating increases in spending in less constrained periods. Earmarking would also help ensure that the health sector would not have to compete with other social sectors in government spending allocation decisions for at least a share of the CREE revenues.

At the same time, some improvements could be made to the current contributory mechanism, in particular towards its simplification. The different framework (with regards to collection, reporting etc.) underlying employee contributions, CREE and the corporate income tax should be harmonised. The potential of these simplification measures to reduce constraints on health revenue raising cannot be overstated: for example, estimates of tax evasion in the corporate income tax in Colombia reach 2.3% of its GDP, thus hinting at a key area for measures aimed at bringing substantial extra resources to health (OECD, 2015). Broader economic policy initiatives seem vital in another area, namely labour market informality. The government's National Development Plan 2010-2014 includes measures aimed at reducing the high rates of informal employment and these should be fully supported – and lobbied for – by the MSPS. Co-ordinated action between the MSPS and other government areas such as the Labour

Ministry is likely to bring dividends in terms of more resources not only to the CR, but also to the SR as informality reductions will tend to raise cross-subsidies from the former to the latter regime as well as enhance the number of enrolees within the SR who contribute financially to the system.

Another alternative for raising additional revenues for the health sector, whose potential would be enhanced by successful initiatives to tame tax evasion and labour informality, is to broaden the range of general taxes earmarked for health. The planned tax on sodas and sugary drinks seems a step in the right direction. Many countries in the OECD and elsewhere have resorted to other earmarked "sin" taxes (for example, having alcohol and cigarette consumption as the basis, activities that contribute to the worrying and expensive burden of some chronic diseases also in Colombia) as a way of increasing the flow of resources to the health system, while at the same time promoting healthy behaviours likely to reduce future treatment costs to the system. Colombia should explore this path while carefully considering the implications for an overall progressive tax structure, again highlighting the need for co-ordinated actions between health authorities and other government ministries.

Explicit definition and adequate costing of publicly funded basic benefits package is a closely linked priority

The equalisation of benefit packages between the SR and CR has been an important step forward to reduce inequalities in the Colombian system. For this step to completely achieved its intended results it is crucial that the quality of services provided in both regimes – which in the past has been perceived as higher for the CR – is indeed brought to a similar standard. Part of the solution for this challenge lies on enhancing the financial and non-financial incentive framework around quality of care facing insurers and providers, as detailed next.

Another set of measures necessary for the real homogenisation of the quality of services offered to SR and CR enrolees relates to restricting the scope for differential exploitation of *tutelas* between regimes – that may favour the more informed and higher income groups normally affiliated to the CR – to translate into different actual benefit packages depending on affiliation. An explicit exclusion list for treatments and therapies in the single basic package (POS) must be outlined as part of this process, based on technical criteria (cost-effectiveness and budget impact) that should be taken into consideration by the courts when deciding on the merit of *tutelas*. The explicit definition of services to be funded with public resources should not be seen as incompatible with a system of universal coverage. Several countries that fund their health systems primarily through taxes or social contributions, ranging from "old" OECD countries like France, Germany and the United Kingdom, to "emerging" economies such as Thailand, Mexico and Costa Rica, have progressed towards ensuring access to necessary care to most of their citizens, while restricting funding to less cost-effective therapies through explicit lists.

The assessment of the costs and benefits of existing and new services as a criterion for the definition of the publicly funded health benefit package is increasingly perceived as a powerful instrument to promote value-for-money and reduce waste, by directly restricting demand for specific interventions whose benefits are not worth the costs. This was a major force behind the creation of several national agencies to assess new technologies in Europe in recent decades, for instance in France, Spain, Sweden and Finland (Mossialos and Le Grand, 1999). The National Institute for Clinical Excellence has long played a major role in assisting resource allocation decisions in the United Kingdom through binding recommendations. In these countries, the recommendations from health technology assessment agencies are used not only to inform the broader definition of the public benefits package (by providing the basis for exclusion of certain therapies with low cost-effectiveness from public funding), but equally to inform decisions about health care guidelines (for example, implementation of pharmaceutical formularies) and cost-sharing schedules (for example, justifying lower or no user charges for cost-effective preventive interventions that reduce the use of more expensive outpatient and inpatient care).

In Colombia, the recent creation of IETS, a health technology assessment agency, should help in this respect but the recommendations provided by this agency should be seen as binding for the allocation of resources, perhaps initially in the case of new technologies and therapies. Ideally, an empowered IETS would be responsible eventually for advising on the updating of the basic package through exclusions and inclusions. The assessment and updating of the POS should be done periodically to ensure access to the most cost-effective services available and deter further growth in *tutelas* and related costs to the system, including inefficient administrative spending by insurers and providers (measures to improve the quality and timeliness of service provision, discussed elsewhere in this chapter, would be equally important to reduce the cost of judicial challenges). It is important that the Colombian authorities ensure that IETS has adequate funds, workforce, political support and international technical assistance to deliver timely, robust and transparent cost-effectiveness assessments. Furthermore, in line with international experiences of technology assessment processes, ensuring transparency and public/patient participation in IETS deliberations will support the credibility of its assessments.

Some countries that have achieved universal coverage have allowed a private insurance market to develop as a supplement to the publicly financed package, offering access to treatments excluded from the public package on a voluntary basis. Examples include Germany, the Netherlands and the United Kingdom, where the pooled financed system is combined with voluntary insurance provision, whereby those who are willing to pay extra can receive other services or enhanced quality of care (through better amenities than in the case of publicly funded services, e.g. individual rooms for hospital stays) (Evans, 2002). This alternative could be adopted in the Colombian context as well subject to careful private insurance regulation by the MSPS regarding aspects such as care quality.

When the POS is redefined as an exclusion list, it becomes even more crucial for the MSPS to ensure that the UPC tariff is adjusted to reflect additional budget impacts, and likewise regularly revised. The need for this constant updating of the UPC in line with updates to the basic package is clear to promote the financial sustainability of providers and insurers, some of which are already experiencing financial distress as discussed above and could see their position deteriorate even further with expansions to the POS. Enhancements to the UPC may be needed to support EPS and IPS dealing with specific population health needs, or engaged in medical research. As an international example that may be a useful model in the Colombian setting, in the Netherlands all taxes and contributions to health are pooled in a centrally-managed risk equalisation fund from which insurers receive risk-adjusted capitation payments. The risk equalisation formula, initially based on simple demographic and epidemiologic information for enrolees, has evolved over time into a sophisticated scheme frequently refined to adequately compensate insurers for differences in case mix and minimise risk selection (Dutch insurers must accept any applicant for the basic insurance policy) (Schut and Van de Ven, 2011).

Improved efficiency through adequate financial and non-financial incentives to system actors will also underpin financial sustainability

One of the areas where Colombia needs urgent reforms is the framework of incentives currently faced by the main actors in the health system. Colombian authorities should draw upon international experience to modify payment systems to EPS, IPS and workforce, in order to increasingly reward quality and outcomes, rather than activity. Piloting of prospective, patient-based reimbursement mechanisms over complete pathways of care, such as the DRG system used in other OECD countries, should begin.

For primary care providers, the development of payment-for-performance mechanisms for general doctors and other professionals has, thus far, been an under-used tool to spur care quality gains. Such mechanisms have been adopted only sporadically through a few local initiatives. A noteworthy example is the case of the Guainía department, whose local government has been piloting a model of public-private partnership for the provision of care that incorporates elements of provider reimbursement tied explicitly to the achievement of pre-determined targets in primary care (mainly coverage of certain services), as discussed in Box 3.1. One of the major disincentives for the development and widespread adoption of pay-for-performance contracts by EPS with IPS and health professionals is the very low level of actual competition between insurers or providers for patients, as discussed throughout Section 2.3.

The implementation of pro-competition measures such as more stringent limits to vertical integration and dissemination of EPS/IPS care quality data should encourage the development of pay-for-performance contracts by EPS in the private sector as a tool to improve quality indicators and attract enrolees. The MSPS should take the initiative by introducing similar workforce reimbursement mechanisms in the network of public providers, as well as encouraging experimentation with tailored pay-for-performance contracting by local governments, through technical and good practice advisory support. In the competitive English setting, for instance, performance-based contracts for primary care clinics and doctors (the *Quality and Outcomes Framework* – QOF) included several primary care targets related to prevention and health promotion (e.g. advice and support for smoking cessation for patients in treatment for diabetes and heart disease), with performance bonuses dependent both on depth of quality in particular areas and breadth of achievement across all indicators in the reward framework. Results have been very positive overall, even for the supply of non-financially incentivised services (Sutton et al., 2010).

Colombia could follow a similar strategy, although the more limited care quality information available points to the need of specifying initially a modest number of priority indicators to be evaluated and determine provider performance. It is important to highlight that payment for performance does not need – and indeed the available evidence indicates it should not – completely replace salaries as a reimbursement mechanism for health professionals. Doctors in the public primary care sector of most OECD countries are paid by a combination of salaries (in many cases including performance-related elements) and capitation (Figueras et al., 2005). Although capitated and pay-for-performance reimbursement methods tend to encourage providers to make process and infrastructure enhancements to attract and keep patients, retrospective mechanisms such as salaries and fee-for-service payments for specific activities may help curb incentives for undersupply of services within capitation reimbursement (McGuire, 2011).

As in primary care, the development of prospective reimbursement mechanisms for hospitals has been hampered too by the weak incentives for quality-driven competition for users. Previously discussed initiatives to strengthen competition based on quality should also encourage the emergence of selective contracting between EPS and IPS and activity-based financing in the private sector. Selective contracting refers to contract models whereby purchasers negotiate with providers around what services are to be provided and under which terms (quality and cost). If models of managed care competition between insurers have resulted in raised system efficiency in different multi-payer contexts such as the Netherlands and the United States, particularly in inpatient care, this has taken place mainly because actual competition for users has been coupled with both selective contracting and payment-for-performance by insurers (Zwanziger et al., 2000; Schut and van de Ven, 2011). Efficiency improvements could be equally expected in the Colombian context if purchasers are faced with the incentive to use selective contracts for strategically choosing a subset of providers and excluding "underperforming" ones.

Selective contracting mechanisms may be easier to implement, initially, with private-sector providers. Overtime, however, quality-based contracting should not be limited to the private sector. EPS in the public sector must also be encouraged to choose strategically from existing public *and* private IPS according to performance, at all levels of care, so as to ensure efficiency and quality gains among public providers in the context of the equalisation of benefit packages between the SR and CR.

In the Colombian public system, much of this incentive should come from the promotion of activity-based financing for hospitals (e.g. DRG-type reimbursement) as a tool to encourage quality-based competition for patients, as opposed to price-based competition. Patient choice coupled with reimbursement based on *ex-ante* fixed tariffs for hospitals led to quality-based competition for patients and care quality improvements in England in the 2000s. This result is in contrast with the situation in the same country during the 1990s, when hospitals were paid through prices negotiated on a case-by-case basis under retrospective reimbursement (and with very limited information available on provider performance). This encouraged hospitals to cut prices through cost reductions, obtained by skimping on quality (Propper et al., 2008). A negative quality effect of price-based competition for patients has also been identified for the hospital market in the United States (Volpp et al., 2003).

The MSPS has a pivotal role to play in the adequate re-alignment of the incentive framework to providers to promote efficiency and quality as described above. Such a role includes the improvement of existing information systems on provider performance (discussed in the next sub-section), as well as the development of effective risk equalisation schemes to be incorporated into the new reimbursement mechanisms. But the MSPS should act beyond these spheres if the goal is to maximise the adoption and potential gains from prospective reimbursement and selective contracting. Efforts on providing effective co-ordination, regulation and oversight of both purchasers and providers will need to be renewed. For instance, while quality-driven competition can be more easily encouraged among public providers (for which the MSPS can set unilaterally a fee schedule with fixed case-based prices and prospective reimbursement), the same outcome in the private sector would require some degree of regulation of hospital prices to avoid situations such as in the English hospital market in the 1990s. Price regulation for private health providers would not be an exclusive feature of the Colombian system by any means; other multiple payer systems (e.g. the Netherlands) have long been regulating the scope of hospital price variation in private markets (Schut and Van de Ven, 2011).

There is currently some perception among actors of the system that EPS could add far more value to the system than is currently the case. The MSPS has an important role in changing the operational framework of public EPS to strengthen their purchasing function, including quality-based contracting with better performing IPS as discussed earlier. This role involves providing support to the EPS with clear contracting guidelines, carefully balanced with adequate autonomy given to them so as to allow the development of innovative purchasing processes. The degree of autonomy awarded to public EPS may vary depending on aspects of their clinical quality, managerial and financial performance, with better performing insurers being rewarded through wider autonomy around generated surpluses and staff hiring, for instance. In such a scenario, the Colombian MSPS should provide technical and operational support to those public EPS that may initially lack basic managerial capacity to function more autonomously, loosening the grip as these payers become more efficient and effective in managing risks and access to services for their enrolled populations, eventually evolving into full-blown strategic purchasers.

Another main area where the re-alignment of current incentives should generate system efficiency gains is pharmaceutical spending. Colombia has made important gains in reducing the prices paid for pharmaceuticals, as explained in Chapter 1, Section 1.5 and Box 1.4. The Dutch case and other international experiences indicate that, while the limits imposed by the Colombian Government on the reimbursement price of drugs have been an important first step to introduce *de facto* limitations on the unpredictable composition and value of the POS, these limits should be revised periodically to adapt to changing market conditions and not discourage innovation.

Periodic revision of pharmaceutical prices is the norm in some OECD countries – including Germany, the Netherlands, New Zealand and Sweden – that have determined maximum or reference reimbursement prices for all drugs with similar therapeutic effects in a particular cluster, usually set based on the lowest priced product in each cluster. The ultimate goal of maximum reimbursement prices in these contexts has been to stimulate price competition and cost savings on pharmaceuticals, with consumers normally required to pay the difference if manufacturers charge prices above the reference price. If implemented judiciously with periodic revisions, there is evidence from the countries mentioned suggesting that reference pricing with ceilings on reimbursement can reduce costs in *both* referenced and non-referenced priced drugs (Moreno-Serra, 2014).

Building on the successes already achieved in controlling pharmaceutical spending, Colombia should follow in the footsteps of these countries by gradually introducing other institutional measures aimed at enhancing the potential of its maximum drug reimbursement policy. Germany and the Netherlands, for instance, opted for introducing mandated generic substitution as another incentive for pharmaceutical companies to reduce prices below the reference price.

Success stories such as New Zealand, where reference pricing has been very effective in reducing costs of pharmaceuticals, are partly based on the requirement by the government – the single purchaser – of price cuts for new generics and their subsequent application to all drugs in the cluster (Danzon and Ketcham, 2004). The market power benefits of a single purchaser situation can be approximated in Colombia by encouraging co-operation within the EPS market in the pharmaceuticals arena, allowing EPS to negotiate as a block for drugs (and potentially other supplies). Joint purchasing and pooling for supplemental rebates could generate reductions in drug manufacturers' prices and lower administrative costs for the EPS through economies of scale, further raising system efficiency.

Improved information systems are needed to promote the efficient allocation of resources

Inefficiencies in resource allocation can only be mitigated if accurate and timely information on aspects such as use of services and provision costs are available to guide MSPS and other actors' planning activities. The system of cost data for public providers needs to be improved and, ideally, integrated with a single reporting system for private institutions, thus consolidating a national system of health accounts to guide efficient resource allocation at all levels. Colombia's system of local and national health accounts needs to be aligned with international norms and facilitate submission of valid and comparable data to frameworks such as the OECD *System of Health Accounts*. It should allow scrutiny of financial flows by providers, insurers, localities, population groups, services and health conditions. Crucially, timely submission of all information requested by the system must be a binding commitment by all actors, ideally enforced by a renewed and stronger supervisory role performed by the *Superintendencia Nacional de Salud*.

Similarly, the scarcity of reliable quality data in the health system is an issue that must be addressed with urgency by Colombian authorities. More and better information needs to be made available for patients on the quality of care provided across the system, through a user-friendly platform and pro-active initiatives by government authorities to disseminate performance results (e.g. through media campaigns), to inform patient choices of care at all levels of complexity. This is a necessary condition for the development of a demanding, selective and transparent performance framework around EPS and IPS as previously advocated, focussed on population health outcomes, quality of care, financial sustainability and administrative capacity. The implementation of the *Choose and Book* and *Quality and Outcomes Framework* systems in England, alluded to above, indicates that an information platform is more likely to succeed in effectively aiding/incentivising patient choice if assisting such choices is made an integral part of doctors' professional responsibilities, and if poor information reporting is linked in practice to financial and legal penalties.

Measures such as those suggested above would contribute to improving the assurance and monitoring of the quality of care across the system, bringing the efficiency levels from the managed competition model closer to those envisaged in the 1993 reform. Enhancing the reporting system and quality of information on financing issues would also help in raising efficiency. As an example, some of the high administrative costs incurred by EPS and IPS because of the current information and reporting infrastructure (see above section on human resources) should be reduced by the simplification of reporting procedures and harmonisation of the cost information system.

2.7. Conclusions

The comprehensive process of health system reforms started by *Ley 100* in Colombia has been the cornerstone of the country's undeterred path towards universal coverage in the last couple of decades. This should be of course a cause for celebration, but the Colombian Government must not become complacent as there are many areas where the initial reforms have created bottlenecks that may prove the undoing of recent successes. This chapter has presented the most pressing challenges ahead in four key health system areas – access to care, care quality, financial sustainability and efficiency issues – and identified policies to address these challenges, whose adoption should be considered a priority by Colombian authorities. Some of these policies have been adopted in other countries with a similar health system configuration to Colombia, offering valuable insights into the path ahead.

Among the system adjustments proposed here, the promotion of real patient choice to improve the quality of care provided, based on the appropriate redesign of the financial and non-financial incentive framework surrounding EPS and IPS, should be paramount. Initiatives that can be more easily implemented in the short-run (more stringent limits to vertical integration between EPS and IPS, for instance) will need to be mixed with more gradual steps in aspects such as movements away from retrospective reimbursement mechanisms for providers and the strengthening of the purchasing function of EPS. As overall system strategy, the recent trend towards the replacement of some contributory pooled funding by general and earmarked taxes for health should continue to be pursued, alongside a more explicit definition of the basic benefit package as an exclusion list to ease financial pressures on actors and the system as a whole.

References

Allemani, C. et al. (2015), "Global Surveillance of Cancer Survival 1995-2009 : Analysis of Individual Data for 25 676 887 Patients from 279 Population-based Registries in 67 Countries (CONCORD-2)", *The Lancet*, Vol. 385, pp. 977-1010.

Amaya Lara, J. et al. (2013), "Estudio de Disponibilidad y Distribución de la Oferta de Médicos Especialistas, en Servicios de Alta y Mediana Complejidad en Colombia (Informe Final)", Documento Técnico GPES/1682C-13, Cendex/Pontificia Universidad Javeriana, Bogotá.

Bernal, O. et al (2013), "The Judicialization of Health in Colombia", *Global Virtual Conference* [online], April 8-12.

Bolivar, M. (2014), "Colombian Health Care System", Presented at "Building systems for Universal Health Coverage: South-South Knowledge Exchange with Korea", December.

Danzon, P. and J. Ketcham (2004), "Reference Pricing of Pharmaceuticals for Medicare: Evidence from Germany, the Netherlands, and New Zealand", in D. Cutler and A. Garber (eds.), *Frontiers in Health Policy Research*, Vol. 7, NBER and MIT Press, Cambridge.

Dávila, C.E. (2015), "Dirección de Financiamiento Sectorial", Personal communication, February 10th 2015, FOSYGA.

Evans, R. (2002), "Financing Health Care: Taxation and the Alternatives", in E. Mossialos, A. Dixon, J. Figueras and J. Kutzin (eds.), *Funding Health Care: Options for Europe*, Open University Press, Buckingham.

Figueras, J., R. Robinson and E. Jakubowski (2005), "Purchasing to Improve Health Systems Performance: Drawing the Lessons", in J. FiguerasJ, R. Robinson and E. Jakubowski (eds.), *Purchasing to Improve Health Systems Performance*, Chapter 3, McGraw-Hill International, Berkshire.

Gaynor, M., R. Moreno-Serra and C. Propper (2013), "Death by Market Power: Reform, Competition, and Patient Outcomes in the National Health Service", *American Economic Journal: Economic Policy*, Vol. 5, pp. 134-166.

Lagomarsino, G. et al. (2012), "Moving Towards Universal Health Coverage: Health Insurance Reforms in Nine Developing Countries in Africa and Asia", *The Lancet*, Vol. 380, No. 9845, pp. 933-943.

McGuire, T. (2011), "Physician Agency and Payment for Primary Medical Care", in S. Glied and P.C. Smith (eds.), *The Oxford Handbook of Health Economics*, Chapter 25, Oxford University Press, Oxford.

Moreno-Serra, R. (2014), "The Impact of Cost-containment Policies on Health Expenditure: Evidence from Recent OECD Experiences", *OECD Journal on Budgeting*, Vol. 12, pp. 1-29.

Moreno-Serra, R. and P.C. Smith (2012), "Does Progress Towards Universal Health Coverage Improve Population Health?", *The Lancet*, Vol. 380, pp. 917-923.

Mossialos, E. and J. Le Grand (1999), "Cost Containment in the EU: An Overview", in E. Mossialos and J. Le Grand (eds.), *Health Care and Cost Containment in the European Union*, Ashgate, Aldershot.

MSPS – Ministry of Health and Social Protection (2013), "Análisis de Situación de Salud según regiones Colombia", Ministerio de Salud y Protección Social, Bogotá.

MSPS (2012), "Encuesta de Evaluación de los Servicios de las EPS", Ministerio de Salud y Protección Social, Bogotá.

Núñez, J. et al. (2012), *La Sostenibilidad Financiera del Sistema de Salud Colombiano*. Fedesarrollo, Bogotá.

OECD (2015), *OECD Economic Surveys: Colombia 2015*, OECD Publishing, Paris.

Orozco Gallo, A. (2014), "Una Aproximación Regional a la Eficiencia y Productividad de los Hospitales Públicos Colombianos", Documentos de Trabajo sobre Economía Regional 201, Banco de la República, Cartagena, March.

PROESA – Research Center for Social Protection and Health Economics (2015), "Cuestión Salud", No. 08, Year 3, February. Available at: www.proesa.org.co (accessed April 15 2015).

Propper, C., S. Burgess and D. Gossage (2008), "Competition and Quality: Evidence from the NHS Internal Market 1991-9", *Economic Journal*, Vol. 118, No. 525, pp. 138-170.

Sarmiento Gómez, A. et al. (2005), "Análisis de eficiencia técnica de la red pública de prestadores de servicios dentro del Sistema General de Seguridad Social en Salud", *Archivos de Economía*, No. 298, Departamento Nacional de Planeación, Bogotá.

Schut, F. and W. van de Ven (2011), "Effects of Purchaser Competition in the Dutch Health System: Is the Glass Half Full or Half Empty?", *Health Economics Policy and Law*, Vol. 6, No. 1, pp. 109-123.

Shekelle, P. (2009), "Public Performance Reporting on Quality Information", in P.C. Smith, E. Mossialos, I. Papanicolas and S. Leatherman (eds.), *Performance Measurement for Health System Improvement: Experiences, Challenges and Prospects*, Chapter 5.2, Cambridge University Press, Cambridge.

Superintendencia Nacional de Salud (2013), "Categorización del Riesgo de las ESE, Vigencia 2011-2012", Superintendencia Nacional de Salud, Bogotá.

Sutton, M. et al. (2010), "Record Rewards: The Effects of Targeted Quality Incentives on the Recording of Risk Factors by Primary Care Providers", *Health Economics*, Vol. 19, No. 1, pp. 1-13.

Uribe, M. (2009), "La dinámica de los actores en la implementación de la reforma del sistema de salud en Colombia: exclusiones y resistencias (1995-2003)", *Revista Gerencia y Políticas de Salud*, Vol. 8, No. 17, pp. 44-68.

van de Ven, W. and F. Schut (2011), "Guaranteed Access to Affordable Coverage in Individual Health Insurance Markets", in S. Glied and P.C. Smith (eds.), *The Oxford Handbook of Health Economics*, Chapter 17, Oxford University Press, Oxford.

Volpp, K. et al. (2003), "Market Reform in New Jersey and the Effect on Mortality from Acute Myocardial Infarction", *Health Services Research*, Vol. 38, pp. 515-533.

Zwanziger, J., G. Melnick and A. Bamezai (2000), "The Effect of Selective Contracting on Hospital Costs and Revenues", *Health Services Research*, Vol. 35, No. 4, pp. 849-867.

Zweifel, P. (2011), "Voluntary Private Health Insurance", in S. Glied and P.C. Smith (eds.), *The Oxford Handbook of Health Economics*, Chapter 13, Oxford University Press, Oxford.

Chapter 3

Primary care in Colombia

Colombia has a good base of policies, institutions, financial and informational frameworks in place to underpin delivery of effective primary care, including in rural and remote areas. The primary care sector is not as strong as it could be, however, and poorer health and access to health care persists in rural and remote areas. Several steps need to be taken if the ambition of having primary care front and centre of the health system, particularly to tackle chronic diseases, is to be realised.

Colombia's first priority must be to collect and publish more information on the quality and outcomes achieved by primary care, in order to benchmark and drive continuous improvement. Transparent reporting of a wider set of quality and outcome measures will enhance the performance and status of the sector and assist in developing a specialist primary care workforce, a closely linked priority. Continued innovation and evaluation of the models of care, especially in rural and remote areas, is also needed.

The statistical data for Israel are supplied by and under the responsibility of the relevant Israeli authorities. The use of such data by the OECD is without prejudice to the status of the Golan Heights, East Jerusalem and Israeli settlements in the West Bank under the terms of international law.

3.1. Introduction

Increasingly over recent years, Colombia's strategic approach to health service delivery has emphasised the central role of primary care. Reforms in 2011 (namely, Law 1438) sought to strengthen universal health coverage by placing preventive and primary care as the cornerstone of the Colombian health system. This Law set out the expectation of an integrated and multidisciplinary approach to primary care, that engaged in risk management, early detection and management of health care needs at individual, family and community level.

Although performance monitoring and improvement have focused less on activities primary care services than in the hospital sector, Colombia is increasingly dedicating resources to address this situation. There are further steps, however, that could be taken to fully equip the primary care sector to play the role expected of it. Improving the availability of quality and outcomes metrics should be a priority. Improving the breadth and transparency of primary care performance data will a key step that allows Colombia to develop a specialist primary care workforce, increase innovation and work toward greater geographic and socioeconomic equality in health and health care access, within a framework of continuous improvement across the whole system.

The chapter is configured as follows. Section 3.2 describes the current state of primary care in Colombia and the strategies implemented. Section 3.3 outlines the disparities in health provision and resourcing in rural and remote areas. Section 3.4 surveys the efforts made to assuring, monitoring and improving the performance of the primary care sector. Section 3.5 assesses the overall state of primary care in Colombia and makes recommendations for improvement.

3.2. The structure of primary care in Colombia

Several reforms in recent years have sought to strengthen the role of primary care in Colombia's health care system. In particular, Law 1438 set out to strengthen universal coverage by emphasising the importance of effective delivery of preventive care and primary care, and reducing demand for more complex and costly secondary health services. The reforms contained in this reform set out the expectation that primary care should be the cornerstone of the Colombian health system.

Primary care is seen as fundamental to tackling Colombia's health care challenges

Colombia's primary care system (*Asistencia Primaria en Salud*, APS) is seen as fundamental to meeting population health care needs. The strategic view of the Ministry of Health is that an effective primary care sector will be vital to improving overall population health, reducing demand for emergency and hospital care, and supporting the financial viability of the health system in the longer term. A governance framework to establish the role of primary care within the wider health system was brought in by Law 1438 of 2011. This set out an expectation of co-ordinated action between government, health care insurers and providers, as well as society, to place APS front and centre of efforts to improve population health. The Law defined APS as an integrated primary care service, capable of delivering quality health services that are inclusive and comprehensive, and situated APS within a broader framework of public health and environmental health efforts. The Law also recognised that targeted initiatives would be needed to strengthen primary care in rural and remote areas, and called upon the government to improve access to health care in these communities and guarantee the necessary resources to finance the provision of health care through public institutions in remote locations.

There is a clear hierarchy of service levels within the Colombian health system, with the primary level serving as the main point of entry into the health system for patients, with the exception of emergency services. Individuals are required to register with an IPS (of their choosing) within their EPS network, and referral from a primary care provider is necessary to access subsequent levels of care. The Ministry of Health has set out an expectation that 90% of complaints should be resolved at primary care level, without the need for referral to secondary care. Primary care providers increasingly work within multidisciplinary teams, including nurses, psychologists, nutritionists and dentists, according to local needs. Some efforts have been made to develop electronic health records for primary care patients, but almost half of APS services still use paper to store patient records.

The vital contribution of primary care services to improved population health in recent years is demonstrated by some key metrics, such as increasing numbers of preventive health care consultations and reductions in maternal and infant mortality. A recent preventive health care consultation was reported by 39% of the population in 1997, rising to 71% in 2010 (MSPS data). Preventive care consultation rates rose most rapidly in the poorest quintile (from 30% to 63% in the same time period), although still lagged behind rates reported by the wealthiest quintile (that rose from 50% to 79%). Figure 3.1 demonstrates steady reductions in maternal and infant mortality between 2005 and 2012.

Figure 3.1. Trends in maternal and infant mortality (per 100 000 births for maternal mortality; per 1 000 live births for infant mortality > 1 year and > 5 years of age)

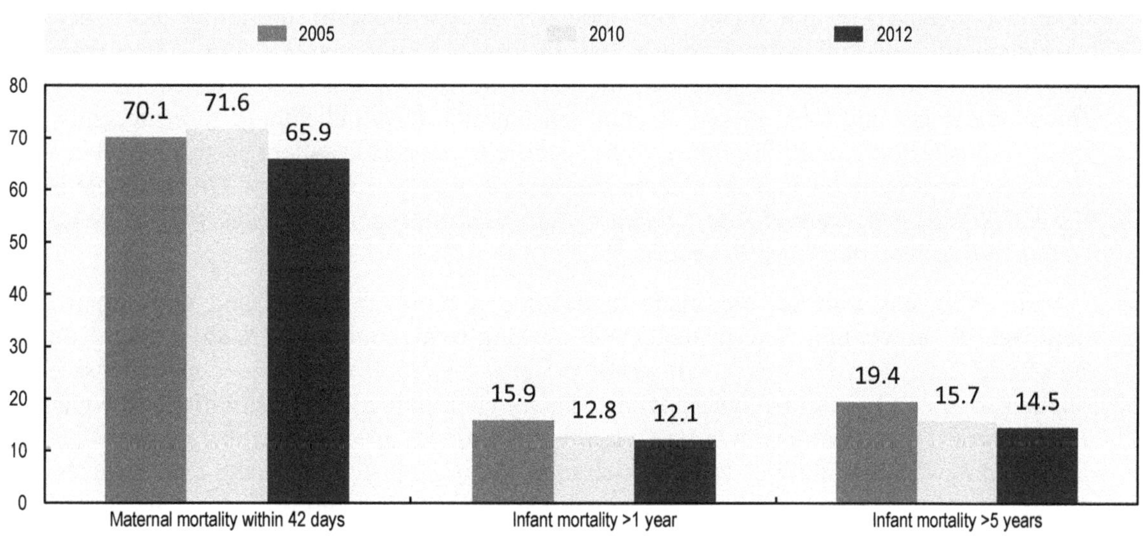

Source: Ministry of Health and Social Protection.

Law 1438 also stressed the role of APS in reducing the burden of non-communicable diseases (NCDs). To this end, the country has engaged with regional and international initiatives such as PAHO's *4x4 Strategy*, that supports implementation of cost-effective preventive interventions to tackle the four main risks factors for NCDs (tobacco, alcohol, unhealthy diet and lack of physical activity). Linked to this, Colombia has adopted the

Sistema de Monitoreo Global de Enfermedades no Transmisibles from WHO. This monitors prevalence and premature mortality from chronic diseases and associated risk factors, and will be used to monitor what local governments are doing to promote healthy lifestyles, as well as the effectiveness of integrated clinical management of non-communicable diseases. This core function of primary care is also reflected in the goals of the National Development Plan (NDP) and Ten Year Public Health Plan, in which specific metrics to assess the impact of primary care are included. The NDP expects by 2021 an increase of 20% in the coverage of prevention and early detection of NCD and seeks to reduce by 25% hypertension in the population over 25 years old.

Integrated care networks focused on long-term conditions are an increasingly important feature of Colombian primary care

A strategic approach to reorienting health services to preventing and managing long-term conditions has, until recently, been lacking in Colombia. Historically, different EPS and IPS developed their own separate models of care, of varying degrees of sophistication and ambition, mostly focused on the treatment and prevention of high cost conditions. Reforms in 2012 (specifically, Resolution 4505) sought to improve prevention and early detection of certain conditions such as cervical and breast cancer, or problems in childhood development, through a programme known as *Protección Específica y Detección Temprana* (PEDT). Clinical guidelines were produced to support these initiatives and, importantly, EPS and IPS are required to report activities related to these PEDT priorities.

Linked to the PEDT initiatives, various risk factors for chronic disease are systematically monitored in primary care. The *Sistema Estándar de Indicadores* (Standard Indicator System, or SEI), has been used in Colombia since 2000, based on criteria established by the WHO. This indicator system monitors mortality, morbidity, socioeconomic determinants of health, risk factors and supply-side factors. Two main categories of indicators are included in the SEI: overweight and physical activity (nine indicators), and tobacco and alcohol consumption (five indicators). More recently, more sophisticated monitoring frameworks specific to particular patient groups have been developed, that include clinical outcome measures as well as risk factors. One example is the OCADER (*Observatorio de Diabetes, Salud Cardiovascular y Enfermedad Renal Crónica*) database, described in Section 3.4.

Colombia has also set out plans to develop a more ambitious and co-ordinated approach to prevention and management of long-term conditions, with a focus on integrated care. The *Política de Atención Integral en Salud* (PAIS, or comprehensive health care policy) aims to better integrate primary care, public health activities and wider intersectoral action at community level. In the PAIS model, primary health care providers are given new responsibilities to be in charge of the organisation of health care services, including individual and collective actions of health promotion and self-care, coverage of specific needs, active search of new cases, early detection, basic treatment and rehabilitation. Enhanced work force capacity and new technologies are also addressed. The model was developed, evaluated and approved through the co-ordination of health professionals, unions, business representatives, academics and international experts. For the time being, PAIS remains, however, largely a set of policy documents. The challenge will be for it to deliver real service reconfiguration on the ground.

Colombia lacks a specialist primary care workforce, although plans are in place to create one

In 2011 there were around 7 700 primary care practitioners and a similar number of hospital specialists working in Colombia. The APS workforce in Colombia, in general, lacks specialist training. After graduating from medical school, Colombian doctors may spend their careers practicing in primary care (or in hospital emergency departments) without any further specialist training. In some cases, employers (whether IPS or EPS) may organise training or education on specific topics for their APS staff, according to local health needs, but this is neither systematised nor particularly incentivised. These loose arrangements persist despite the fact that a recognised speciality of family medicine has existed since the 1980s, comprising three years' postgraduate training. Seven medical schools (the majority in Bogotá) offer this programme, but less than 500 doctors have taken it up over the past three decades.

A number of reasons for the low popularity of primary care specialist training have been suggested. First, doctors in Colombia must pay out-of-pocket for any postgraduate training they undertake. Second, specialist training is not compulsory to practice as a primary care doctor. Third, salaries and working conditions in APS services are generally recognised to be of poor quality, limiting the incentives to pursue this career path. One study looking at public providers found that specialists were paid almost 25% higher salaries than generalists (Sarmiento Gómez et al., 2005). Employment contracts for primary care doctors are typically for six months or less. As a result, APS services are characterised by a high turnover of staff, disruptive both for services and the professionals themselves. Most importantly, however, it prevents creation of a sustained, continuous relationship between individual patients and doctors, which is a fundamental feature of high quality primary care.

Colombia's Ministry of Health recognises that modern primary care requires a specialist workforce that benefit from continuing professional development and attractive working conditions. Law 1164 in 2007 defined core professional competencies for APS (as well as other clinical specialities), which were later embedded in the PAIS model of primary care delivery. More recently, the ministry has taken further steps to specify a training curriculum, at both undergraduate and postgraduate level, to reinvigorate the speciality of family medicine , through which the ministry intend to create 5 000 family medicine specialists over ten years. This will depend on successful co-operation with Colombia's medical schools, who are largely autonomous. The curriculum places strong emphasis on preventive, continuous and person-centred health care. Thirty medical schools across Colombia now offer a one-year postgraduate course in family medicine.

3.3. Provision of primary care in rural and remote Colombia

Differences in the levels of health care resources are still very apparent when comparing provision of primary care in rural and remote areas to urban areas. Differences in population health outcomes are, however, less that might be expected. Nevertheless, it is recognised that a different delivery and financing model is needed in rural and remote areas in order to achieve levels of access and quality that are comparable to more urban settings. Although several initiatives have been introduce to enable this, relatively little innovation has taken place on the ground.

Health care resources and access to care remain worse in rural and remote areas

Although an increasing majority of its residents lives in urban populations (76% in 2014, projected to reach 84% by 2050), there is still a significant share of Colombians that live in rural and remote areas (RRA), for whom access to health care services remains limited. The remoteness of some populations, in addition to the precarious state of roads, high transportation costs, and the lack of an articulated supply of health services, act as barriers to entry for the rural and indigenous population. In addition to these barriers to entry, unequal resourcing remains a problem, evidenced by the lack of medical facilities, supplies and human resources in RRAs.

Relative under-resourcing compared to other parts of Colombia remains a problem for these populations. The density of generalist (primary care) doctors, varies from less than 2.5 per thousand population in the departments of Chocó, Guanía, Vaupés and Vichada to over 17.0 in the departments of Bogotá/Cundinamarca, Risaralda, Santander and Valle del Cauca (2013 data). Stark differences are also seen in secondary care services. Around one third of all secondary care specialists work from Bogota. For psychiatry, the imbalance is even worse. Of the total number of psychiatrists in the country 49.7% live in Bogota.

Figure 3.2. Available beds per 1 000 people by district, 2014

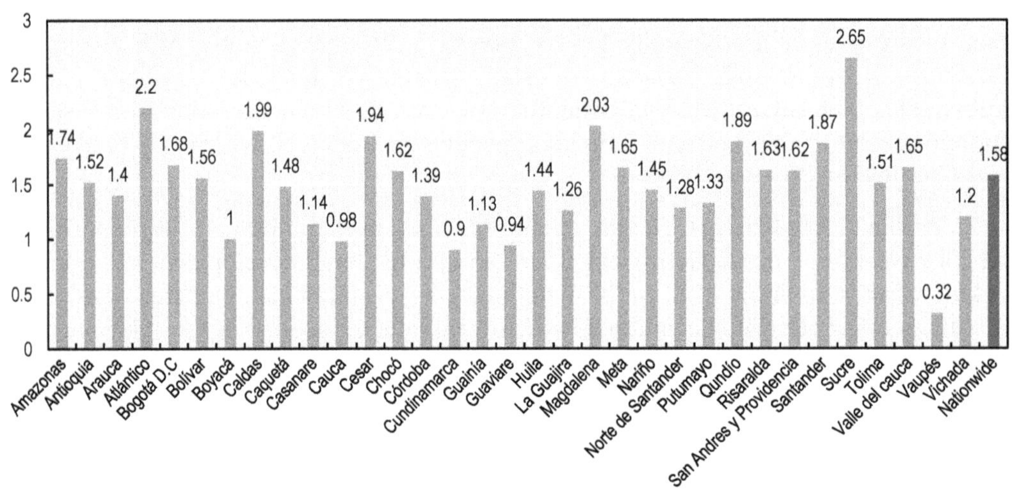

Source: Ministry of Health and Social Protection.

The distribution of hospital beds also reflects disparities in access and resources. As shown in Figure 3.2, available beds per 1 000 inhabitants ranges from 0.32 to 2.65, with a national mean of 1.58, which is very low in comparison to the OECD average of 4.8 per 1 000 inhabitants. Moreover rural populations such as Vaupés, Cundinamarca, Guaviare and Cauca have even less than 1 bed per 1 000 inhabitants (OECD, 2015a). When grouping municipalities by size, the differences are more evident; district capitals register an average density of 2.24 beds per 1 000 inhabitants, whilst small municipalities with less than 100 000 inhabitants have a bed density of only 0.79 per 1 000 inhabitants.

A similar picture characterises the distribution of surgical facilities throughout the country (Figure 3.3). Nationally, there are 6.27 operating rooms per 100 000 inhabitants. In densely populated localities, such as Atlántico and San Andrés y Providencia, this figure can reach ten or more surgical facilities per 100 000 inhabitants, while most rural populations are below national mean. In particular, this indicator is alarmingly low (under 3) in six entities (Casanare, Chocó, Cundinamarca, Guaviare, Vaupés and Vichada) that do not even reach half the national average.

Figure 3.3. Available operating rooms per 100 000 people by district, 2014

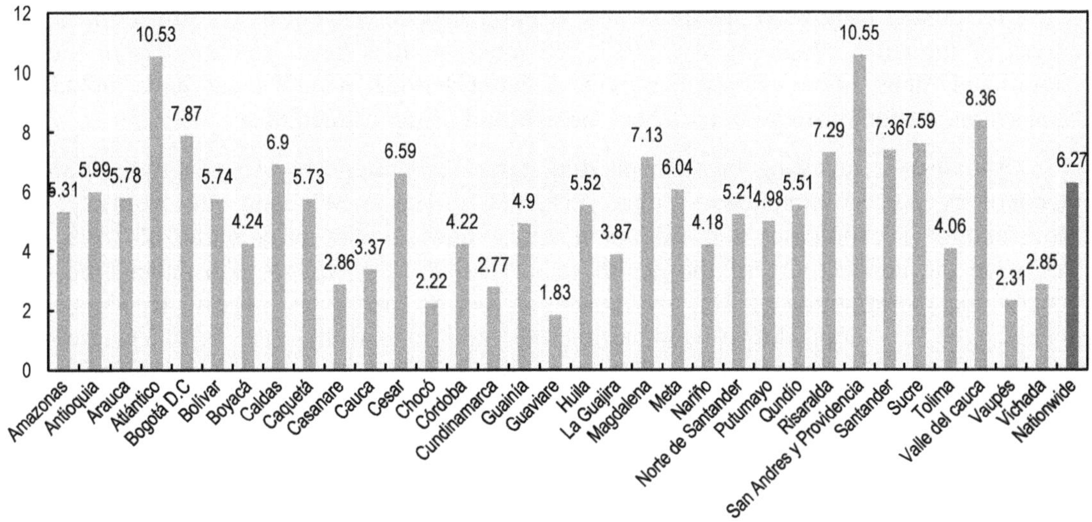

Source: Ministry of Health and Social Protection.

Detailed health needs assessments in RRA, as well as Colombia more widely, have been carried out for several years. These gather information on reported health status, mental well-being, access to nutrition, environmental health, occupational health and social support networks. These surveys are used to try and better allocate resources for local health needs, within the overall aim of reducing geographic and socioeconomic inequalities in health and health care. In addition, health service user-surveys, such as the *Encuesta de Evaluación de los Servicios de las EPS*, allow beneficiaries to evaluate the services received from their EPS, is another effort to assess the differences in quality of care provided by regions. Small sample sizes can limit the usefulness of findings, however.

Surveys such as these help quantify differences in access, quality and outcomes of health care across urban and rural populations. These differences are reducing and are not, perhaps, as great as might be expected. In urban populations, for example, 1.8% of children aged under two years of age are recorded as never having received any vaccinations, compared to 1.0% rural children. Similarly, 26.1% of urban children aged under four years were found to be anaemic in 2010, comparted to 30.8% of rural children. Concerning maternal health, 99% of births in urban areas are attended by a trained health care worker, compared to 94% in rural and remote areas. Nevertheless, in Colombia's 2011 quality of life survey, 16% of the rural population reported foregoing health care needs because of the distance to services, compared to 2.3% of the urban population (ECV, 2011) signalling an on-going need to improve access to care for the former group.

Innovations in the rural health care delivery model are relatively few, however, apart from expanding use of telemedicine

Colombia takes the problem of inequalities in health and in access to health care services seriously. Since the inception of the SGSSS with Law 100, additional resources have been targeted to rural, remote and indigenous populations, aimed to compensate both for greater health care needs as well as the increased costs of delivering services in areas of limited accessibility. By 2013, 363 municipalities have benefitted from these additional funds. Other efforts to provide a better service in rural areas have included translating health information into local dialects and using telemedicine.

Colombia is investing in an expanding range of options to use new information technology and communication platforms (ITC). The MSPS and the Ministry of Information Technologies and Communications have a joint programme of work to improve the connectivity of the health sector called *Vive Digital*. This plan aims to encourage the adoption of ITC in health services. In particular, health providers are encouraged to adopt digital medical records and extend the use of telemedicine. According to 2014 data (*Encuesta de Línea Base de Telemedicina*), the vast majority of IPS have some capabilities for tele-consultation, and this has emerged as a useful tool to improve access to primary care services in remote populations at a moderate cost, but must expand its usage throughout the country in order to be truly effective.

In addition, both Law 1438 and the developing PAIS model acknowledge the need for a differentiated delivery of care in different regions. In particular, it is recognised that rural and remote areas require a supply-led model of health care, rather than the demand-led model of managed competition that was prioritised by the 1993 reforms. On the ground, however, it appears that relatively little innovation has occurred, other than modest efforts to translate information into local dialects or use telemedicine as described above. One exception is the recently approved pilot for community-led health care delivery in the Guainía region, with the support of the Inter-American Development Bank (see Box 3.1). There are no formal policies in place governing the recruitment and retention of primary care doctors in RRA. However, the MSPS has designed a strategy to optimise the assignation process of doctors that aims for a better distribution throughout the country, improving coverage in rural and remote areas. The strategy includes flexibility in hiring conditions, as well as a gradual improvement of wages and result based incentives that aim to encourage primary care clinicians to take up posts in these areas.

Box 3.1. Rural health care provision in Guainía

Guainía is a remote province where over 85% of the population is indigenous. A pilot programme, within the PAIS framework, was recently launched that seeks to improve quality and access of primary care services in the province. A single insurer/single provider delivery model has been developed, based upon a public-private partnership with both demand- and supply- side subsidies, including pay-for-performance. Close involvement of local indigenous communities in the objectives and design of the model was a prominent part of the initiative. In particular, knowledge from the indigenous communities and traditional health practices are legally and structurally incorporated into the primary care service delivery model. This local contextualisation is seen as particularly important in the implementation of health promotion and preventive care strategies, starting from family and community levels.

3.4. Assuring, monitoring and improving the performance of primary care in Colombia

Primary care services have, historically, received less investment in performance monitoring and improvement activities compared to the hospital sector in Colombia, as across all OECD health systems. The country is now, however, devoting significant attention to correcting this. Minimum quality standards are in place for APS, alongside a limited set of clinical guidelines. Nevertheless, there is still a marked lack of data on primary care outcomes and a need to focus performance-monitoring activities on the rapidly developing challenge of chronic illnesses such as diabetes.

Minimum quality standards and accreditation pathways for primary care exist, but seem to be designed with hospital, rather than APS, services in mind

Colombia's *Sistema Obligatorio de Garantía de Calidad de la Atención en Salud* (SOGC, or obligatory health care quality assurance system) is a fairly comprehensive set of tools that seeks to assure, monitor and improve health care quality. It comprises four elements: i) the *Sistema Único de Habilitación*, which is a set of minimum financial and technical specifications that must be met in order to be recognised as a health care provider; ii) the *Sistema Único de Acreditación* a voluntary accreditation system, which identifies institutions performing beyond the basic requirements of the *Sistema Único de Habilitación*; iii) audit programmes, which seek to drive continuous quality improvement, for specific clinical activities (such as vaccination) or specific patient groups (such as pregnant women); and iv) the *Observatorio de Calidad de la Atención en Salud*, which is an information system that allows public reporting and benchmarking across EPS and IPS, and encourages continuous quality improvement.

Achieving accreditation through the *Sistema Único de Acreditación* brings health care providers certain benefits such as higher tariffs or priority access to schemes to support international marketing, as well as reputational enhancement. Accreditation requirements place particular emphasis on preventive health care and early detection of conditions such as cancer, cardiovascular disease and diabetes. Providers need to have programmes in place to systematically offer such prevention and early detection, especially for new patients. Providers are required to offer these activities as part of an integrated programme of person-centred health care, and audit their success in doing so.

Colombia's accreditation system appears to be an effective means of promoting preventive care. Of note, however, the SOGC applies to all health services, and seems particularly designed with hospital services in mind. Even though the accreditation system has a distinct and dedicated pathway for ambulatory care, much of it refers to out-patient services, day-case surgery and diagnostic/laboratory services – signalling the hospital-centric thinking underpinning it. An accreditation, and broader quality assurance, framework that takes APS services as its main focus is currently lacking in Colombia.

An increasing number of clinical guidelines exist, but these do not always set out what specifically is expected of primary care

The Ministry of Health has published several clinical guidelines to support the delivery of primary care, with a focus on prevention and early detection. These include guidelines around family planning, management of pregnancy and birth, childhood development and growth, oral health and vaccination. More recently, a number of *Guías de Atención Integral* (GAI, or guidelines for integrated care) have been produced in association with local universities. These cover topics such as safe childbirth, childhood illnesses and sexually transmitted infections.

Increasingly, these documents cover non-communicable chronic diseases. Several clinical guidelines address various cancers, cardiovascular disease and chronic lung disease, for example. Guidelines are also available for depression, alcohol abuse and schizophrenia. Although it is recognised that primary care must be at the forefront of efforts to reduce the burden of these illnesses, Colombia's clinical guidelines do not always set out what specifically is expected of primary care in terms of prevention, detection and management. The guideline of chronic obstructive pulmonary disease, for example, makes no special mention of primary care. An exception is the guideline on depression, which has a section dedicated to the role of APS. It makes a strong recommendation, for example, that mild episodes of depression should be fully managed within primary care. More broadly, however, recognition of the distinct role that APS should fill in tackling NCDs is lacking.

Activity and outcomes data is relatively lacking in primary care

Beyond the high-level measures around preventive care consultations presented in Section 3.2, a more detailed picture of quality and value-for-money in the sector, or of the performance of individual APS providers, is lacking. A significant volume of data around APS services is routinely collected, but most of it pertains to inputs, activities and costs. The core information system underpinning APS is the *Registro Individual de Prestación de Servicios de Salud* (RIPS, or register of individual health services). It holds basic demographic information on individuals, their diagnoses and linked health care activities. RIPS is primarily an administrative database, designed to monitor delivery of the POS and facilitate contracting between insurers and providers. Clinical outcomes and other quality measures do not feature.

The *Observatorio de Calidad de la Atención en Salud* contains some indicators relevant to APS (see Table 1.1 in Chapter 1). The majority of these are process measures, such as accessibility of appointments or timeliness of cervical cancer screening or childhood vaccination. Promisingly, some outcome measures relevant to APS are reported, although these remain few in number. They comprise the proportion of patients with hypertension whose blood pressure is controlled, and the rate of readmission to hospital after discharge (each reported by IPS); and mortality rate after pneumonia, and maternal mortality rate (each reported by EPS). Patient satisfaction measures are also collected (reported by both IPS and EPS), and these show that 80% of service users reported having been served always/almost always with kindness and respect by administrative personnel and 85% by health care personnel.

Broadly, few primary care indicators refer to outcomes, and fewer still to chronic diseases. Importantly, even available data does not appear to be currently well used. The website of the *Observatorio de Calidad* (calidadensalud.minsalud.gov.co) is intended to provider peer comparison of EPS and IPS performance on these indicators. Tabular, graphical and map-based interfaces are offered. In practice, however, few results are available and some appear to lack validity (the pneumonia mortality rate for children less under five, for example, is reported to have been 0.02 in 2012 and 2.73 in 2013; no units are given[1]). Some EPS are developing mechanisms to provide their IPS network with feedback on their performance and individual disease registers/observatories are introducing benchmarking systems (such as the Observatory for the Prevention and Management of Chronic Renal Failure). In general, however, a national approach to primary care performance management is lacking. As a result, incentives to deliver better primary care remain weak.

Colombia has begun to develop a number of public health observatories and national surveys. These are not, however, true patient or disease registers, and few of them are directly linked to primary care. The National Cancer Observatory, to give one example, publishes mortality rates but these data are drawn from national surveys, not from APS providers. They give some indication of the combined impact of APS, public health and other interventions at municipal, departmental and national level, but are of limited use in understanding the effectiveness of individual APS providers. In addition, cancer mortality is heavily determined by prevalence of the disease and cancer outcomes are not considered as falling within the ambit of primary care in most health systems. Broadly, however, most primary care indicators still refer to maternal and child health, not chronic diseases. Hence the country is limited in its ability to develop more valid metrics of primary care quality.

An exception to this appears to be the recently established *Observatorio de Salud Cardiovascular, Diabetes y Enfermedad Renal Crónica* (Observatory for Cardiovascular Health, Diabetes and Chronic Renal Disease, or OCADER). These are chronic conditions well within the remit of primary care. The Observatory will collect a range of indicators, including key clinical outcomes such as proportion of diabetic patients with inadequately treated hypertension or elevated blood cholesterol. Results disaggregated to regional/municipal level will be available, but it is unclear whether APS providers will be benchmarked against each other.

3.5. Strengthening primary care in Colombia

Colombia has a good base of policies, institutions, financial and informational frameworks in place to underpin delivery of effective primary care. Several steps now need to be taken, however, if the ambition of having APS at the front and centre of tackling chronic disease is to be realised. Colombia's first priority must be to collect and publish more information on the quality and outcomes achieved by primary care, in order to drive continuous improvement. Transparent benchmarking of quality and outcomes will enhance the status of the sector and assist in developing a specialist primary care workforce, another key priority. Continued innovation in the models of care, especially in rural and remote areas, is also needed.

A richer information system should underpin incentives toward better APS performance, eventually including innovations in payment mechanisms

Not enough is known about the activities, costs and outcomes of primary care in Colombia. Development of more effective monitoring of primary care quality and outcomes is a priority because APS services currently have very few incentives to improve performance. Hence, a richer information system, with a focus on the outcomes achieved by primary care, should be Colombia's first priority to strengthen the sector. Given Colombia's epidemiologic transition, the focus, initially, should be on quality and outcomes for key chronic conditions such as obesity, diabetes and cardiovascular disease, as well as mental health. Validated metrics of the quality of primary care for these conditions are well established internationally (such as rates of avoidable hospitalisation), and should be adopted by Colombia.

The model being developed within PEDT, where EPS and IPS are required to report activities related to prevention and early detection activities, provides a nucleus for something that could develop into a sophisticated monitoring system – if the focus shifts to collecting outcomes as well as activities. As described earlier, Colombia's SISPRO and SOGC databases are excellent platforms from which to build further. The emphasis must now be on defining, collecting and analysing more quality and outcome measures linked to APS services. Most other OECD health systems are rapidly developing in this area, and can point to how richer primary care outcomes data has led to service improvements. Israel's *Quality Indicators in Community Healthcare* programme is a particularly well-known example. It is appealing because of its relative simplicity, yet proven benefit in driving service improvements. Other models would be the DAK-E system in Denmark, or the *Quality and Outcomes Framework* in the United Kingdom (OECD, 2013a).

Once indicator definitions and data collection/analysis capabilities are in place, Colombia should then move to ensure that it has complete coverage of the relevant denominator populations, by developing a fuller set of patient registers (for example, by registering all diabetics in Colombia). A more extensive set of local or national patient registers should be developed therefore. This work need not necessarily fall to the Ministry of Health. Clinicians or academics with specialist knowledge of particular clinical areas, and a passion to improve health care in Colombia, should be invited to lead programmes to develop patient registers and linked quality metrics. Colombia should make full advantage it has in the SISPRO database, by ensuring that all patient registers are compatible in their contents and format from the outset. Other countries with long histories of patient registers (often developed spontaneously by pioneering clinicians), now find themselves struggling to achieve compatibility and a strategic approach across them. It is essential that Colombia avoid this difficulty by developing a modular approach, within a common SISPRO framework, from the outset.

Box 3.2. Israel's Quality Indicators in Community Healthcare programme

The Israeli experience is particularly informative here. As mentioned, Israel is of particular interest because of the existence of four health funds, each vertically linked to provider networks, in a system which resembles that of Mexico. The four funds can boast impressive reforms over the past decade that have helped consolidate primary care services into teams and improved support for patients living with chronic disease. Health funds also play an active role in driving continuous improvement in the quality of care based on a broad range of data on whether good practices are being undertaken and what patient outcomes are. The sum of these efforts is that among OECD countries, Israel's health system is particularly good at identifying chronic diseases amongst patients early and supporting those living with a health condition to avoid an unnecessary hospital visit. Diabetes care is a revealing example of the good performance of Israeli health system. Efforts by the government to prevent and control diabetes have contributed to low number of admissions to hospitals for uncontrolled diabetes among OECD countries, while reductions in complications demonstrate ongoing efforts to improve quality of care provided to patients with diabetes (OECD, 2012).

Israel's National Programme for Quality Indicators in Community Healthcare (QICH) has been instrumental in delivering these gains. The QICH programme captures more than 35 measures of quality of care on preventive measures, use of recommended care and the effectiveness of care. The data is available for almost the entire population according to age, sex and a proxy for socio-economic status. The QICH is an important resource for quality improvement activities undertaken by the four insurer/provider bodies in Israel. They draw on the QICH data to benchmark their own performance and identify potential shortfalls. Insurer/providers have developed innovative programmes including patient education and empowerment initiatives and have also developed targeted programmes to deliver greater access to high quality care specific patient groups (OECD, 2012).

Box 3.2. Israel's Quality Indicators in Community Healthcare programme *(cont.)*

The structure of the Quality Indicators in Community Healthcare (QICH) programme, Israel

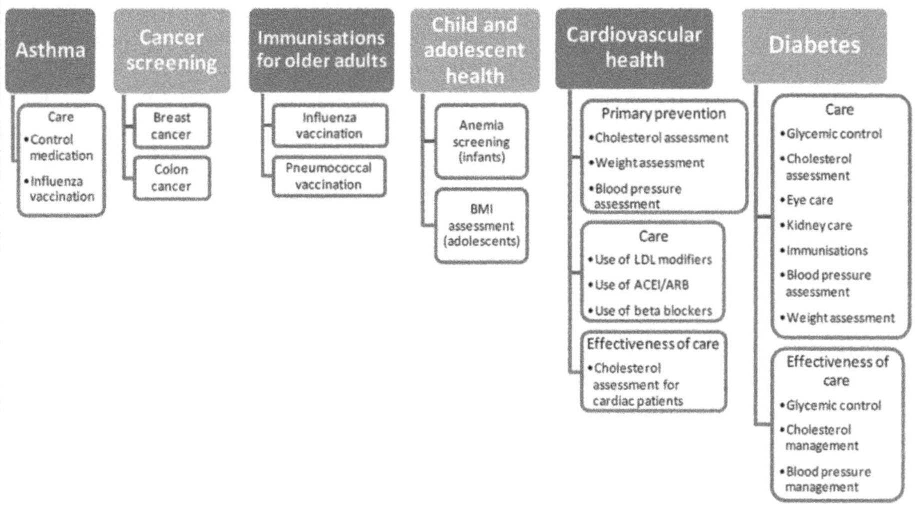

Source: OECD (2012), *OECD Reviews of Health Care Quality: Israel 2012: Raising Standards*, OECD Publishing, http://dx.doi.org/10.1787/9789264029941-en.

Once there is greater confidence in the coverage of denominator populations and the validity of the indicators, an active programme of audit and research should be encouraged, with a focus on transparent comparison of providers' results. Again, clinicians and academics should be encouraged to lead this work, with government authorities taking strategic oversight – particularly to ensure that findings lead to service improvement, nationally and locally. Comparing the performance of Colombian APS services against international peers (through the OECD *Health Care Quality Indicators* programme) will be an important signal of the system's maturity.

Variation within Colombia across EPS and IPS should be also studied closely, both as a means to improve performance overall as well as tackle inequalities. Results on APS services' comparative performance should be readily available to EPS and IPS, since this kind of feedback is currently lacking in Colombia. Colombia may wish to restrict benchmarking results to professional groups initially but, as confidence in the validity of metrics grows, findings should be made available to the public. This would serve as a strong driver to improve performance, and is particularly important in a system such as Colombia's where patient choice is seen as an integral part of system design. Work is underway to make SISPRO's health system information more accessible, to both professionals and the public, through an internet portal that allows generation of charts, graphs and maps. This work should continue. The way primary care performance metrics are fed back to individual General Practitioners within Denmark's DAK-E system is a good example of information being used to drive continuous quality improvement that Colombia could aspire to.

Box 3.3. Denmark's DAK-E initiative

The approach taken to demonstrating and improving value for money in Danish primary care is informative. In Denmark, a system of automatic data capture, commonly referred to as DAMD, includes diagnoses, procedures, prescribed drugs and laboratory results. Since April 2011 every practice has become obliged to participate. GPs can access quality reports from their own practice for the management of chronic diseases including diabetes and heart failure, as well as other clinical areas of primary care practice. An example of the feedback available to them, in this case relating to diabetes management, is shown in below. The system enables easy identification of individual patients who are treated sub-optimally and also allows them to benchmark their practice against other practices. Analyses examining the quality of diabetes primary care reported significant improvements in the proportion of diabetics on anti-diabetic, antihypertensive and lipid-lowering medications (OECD, 2013a). A key observation is that neither DAMD is not linked to financial incentives – it is the informational or reputational incentive alone which drives better performance across Danish primary care providers. This is also true for Israel's QICH, described in Box 3.2.

DAMD output allowing GPs to compare the quality of their practice with peers

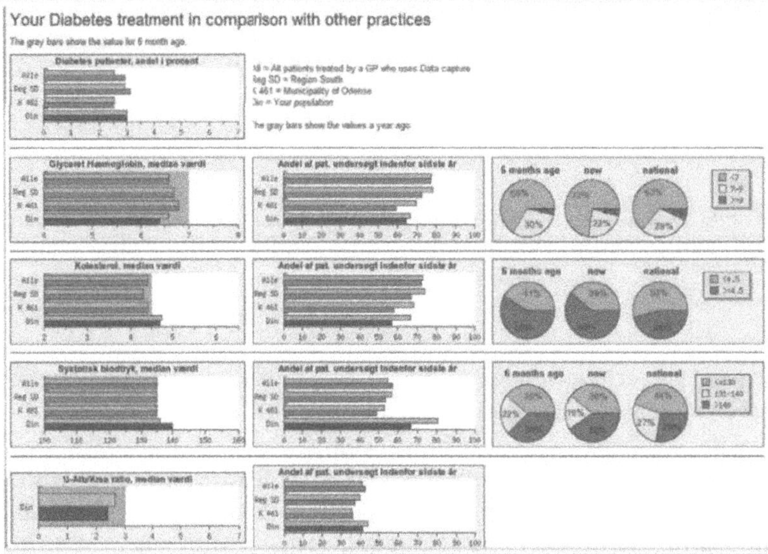

Glossary: *Median værdi*: median value; *andel af pat. undersøgt indenfor sidste år*: proportion of patients with an annual check in the last 15 months.

Source: www.dak-e.dk.

Within Colombia, the model being developed by the OCADER observatory signals a promising way forward. The Observatory will collect a range of indicators, including key clinical outcomes such as proportion of diabetic patients with inadequately treated hypertension or elevated blood cholesterol. Results disaggregated to regional/municipal level will be available, but it is unclear whether APS providers will be benchmarked against each other.

A solid body of standards, guidelines, quality indicators and analysis of variance will allow Colombia to establish an accreditation pathway specific to APS. Accreditation for excellence pathways exist for ambulatory care, but these do not reflect the objectives and activities of APS services well. Developing a tailored APS accreditation process will enhance the status of the sector, as well as encourage excellence and continuous quality improvement.

Finally, once confidence in the validity and comparability of performance metrics is established, Colombia should move to link them to payment for APS services. Currently, these are mainly paid for through fee-for-service (FFS) and capitation, which may limit the incentives towards achieving better outcomes. Many OECD health systems are moving towards blended payment systems for primary care that include pay-for-performance (P4P) elements, in an effort to more clearly reward quality and outcomes, rather than just activity. In Colombia, the Ministry of Health has recently commissioned work to explore the feasibility of including P4P in how Colombia pays for APS services, and work on incentivising some aspects of the detection and management of chronic renal failure has started. Continued discussions and piloting of innovations should be encouraged, at both local and national level. OECD primary care systems demonstrate a wealth of models that Colombia could consider, Portugal being a particularly sophisticated example (see Box 3.4). Japan offers a contrasting example. There, FFS has been retained as the dominant payment mechanism, but in an unusually detailed and dynamic manner, such that providers' activities closely follow health system priorities.

Box 3.4. Pay-for-Performance in Portuguese Family Health Units

In 2005, the Portuguese Ministry of Health started the restructuring of traditional health care centres into small autonomous functional units (teams of family doctors, nurses and clinical secretaries), known as Family Health Units (FHU). As part of the reform, newly formed FHUs had different payment mechanisms than the traditional GP clinics (Primary Health Care Centres), in which GPs were salaried. FHUs are paid through a mix of capitation, fixed bonuses, and pay for performance (P4P).

Context and problem the reform aims to address

The Portuguese NHS performs well (OECD, 2015b), but was considered to have a highly centralised and bureaucratic structure, with few incentives for good performance or quality. Job dissatisfaction for primary care practitioners, paid with fixed salaries, was an area for concern. Primary health care centres were also seen as too large for providing care, taking into account the provision of services with proximity and quality, and too small for the purpose of economies of scale, achieving efficiency gains and improvements in management. The Government Programme (2005-2009) for health gave special emphasis to primary care, and was followed by the creation of a Primary Health Care Task Force with the aim of conducting an overall reform of primary care, including the implementation of Family Health Units. In September 2014, 47.82% of the Portuguese citizens were enrolled with an USF. Traditional primary health care centres continue to serve citizens not enrolled in a USF.

Understanding the payment reform

FHUs are small multi-professional teams, which are formed of self-selecting family doctors (up to 8) along with an equal number of family nurses and clinical secretaries, covering from 4 000 to 14 000 people. The creation of new USF was facilitated by substantial financial support in the setting up of facilities, IT and general work conditions. The new primary care payment scheme was exclusively developed for FHU. Two different models – Model A and Model B – of FHU have been established (a third model, Model C, has not been operationalised), which have differing degrees of organisational autonomy, different legal statuses, and different funding and incentive models.

- Model A: all FHUs start as Model A FHUs, and must prove that they are meeting specific quality, clinical and functional targets before they are allowed to apply to transition to Model B. All of the Model A FHU's personnel remuneration is governed by the public administration's legislation for the correspondent sector and career (e.g. legislation affecting GP salary, family nurse salary). Within Model A FHUs there is scope to negotiate the provision of additional services, and to receive additional remuneration for these services. Model A FHUs can also negotiate with the contracting agency (typically the ACES/Regiona) to agree a certain set of objectives, the achievement of which leads to additional financial incentives which are shared between the FHU team.

Box 3.4. Pay-for-Performance in Portuguese Family Health Units *(cont.)*

- Model B: FHUs can progress from Model A to Model C, with the approval of the relevant ACES/Region. The remuneration process for Model B FHUs has two components: a fixed component and a variable one. The fixed component corresponds to the legislated remuneration (GP salary, nurse salary, etc.), while the variable component is based on all of the supplementary payments that the FHU can receive derived from the individual health professionals' performance, and the unit's results, across a selection of performance indicators. Model B FHU have a fairly significant payment mix, including salary, adjusted capitation, FFS, and P4P.

For Model B FHUs, financial incentives to nurses and clinical secretaries are similar, and are dependent on patient's list (adjusted capitation), opening hours and achievement degree of contracted health indicators. Besides a basic salary, family doctors financial incentives depend on the patient's list (adjusted capitation), home visits (fee for service until a maximum of 20 visits per month), pay for performance (i.e. correct surveillance of: women in reproductive age; pregnancy; infant within the first year; infant within the second year; patient with diabetes; patient with high blood pressure) and other components (i.e. supplement for USF co-ordination, supplement for training interns) or additional activities (e.g. smoke cessation).

Initially, contracting only consider 15 national indicators to USF Model A (used to apply team financial incentives) and 14 indicators to USF Model B (used to apply team financial incentives to nurses and clinical secretaries). The definition of targets depended on the negotiations between USF and RHA representative and should take into account the behaviour of the indicators in each USF and surrounding health centres. In 2014, following public open discussion and negotiations with different trade unions, indicators and achievement measurement were changed. Targets were to be set based on 22 contracted indicators, selected from a national set of more than 100 indicators. Targets are defined by national heath objectives, good practices, available resources and historical data.

Assessing the payment reform

The reform has been analysed a number of times, by different bodies. In 2009, EUROPEP (a 23-item validated instrument and internationally standardised measure of patient evaluations of general practice care) survey was applied to 16 768 patients (12 713 respondents), by an academic institution, which showing a global level of patient satisfaction with FHU of 73.2%, with 86% of the individuals very or extremely satisfied with the provision of care. Another study conducted in 2009 analysed professionals satisfaction (2 398 respondents); 72.2% considered the FHU as high quality working place.

The Portuguese Court of Auditors carried out an audit for period encompass from 2006 and 2012. This audit was very controversial and almost all stakeholders contested their conclusions. Still, the Court of Auditors concluded that the FHU model shows, on average, greater economic efficiency, in the unit cost per medical consultation or user, when compared with traditional primary health care centres, which have higher unit costs.

The Regional Health Authorities and the Central Administration for the Health System produce annual reports showing the results achieved by FHU and traditional primary health care centres. Invariably, FHU achieve better access to care, clinical performance and higher efficiency. For example, recent data from 2013 show that hypertensive patients and diabetics are better controlled by USF than traditional health care centres:

- Proportion of controlled diabetics:
Traditional primary health care centres: 41.5%
FHU Model A: 61.6%
FHU Model B: 70.3%
- Proportion of hypertensive patients with controlled blood pressure
Traditional primary health care centres: 37,8%
FHU Model A: 53.8%
FHU Model B: 65.2%

Source: OECD (2015), *OECD Reviews of Health Care Quality: Portugal 2015: Raising Standards*, OECD Publishing, Paris, http://dx.doi.org/10.1787/9789264225985-en.

A specialist primary care workforce should be developed, focused on tackling the rising tide of chronic conditions such as diabetes

A stronger, more transparent, primary care performance management system, generating evidence of population health benefit, will lead to a more professionalised sector, with higher status. A distinct and specialist primary care workforce will be essential to realising Colombia's ambitions of placing APS at the centre of efforts to prevent and manage chronic diseases. In addition to a richer information infrastructure, other steps will also need to be taken.

An important initial step in this direction would be to develop standards and guidelines specific to APS services. As described earlier, there are currently few standards and guidelines to support the prevention and management of chronic conditions, which specifically address the role of APS. A more extensive set of APS-specific standards and guidelines, focussed on chronic diseases should be developed. These can be expected to have several, mutually reinforcing benefits. First, standards and guidelines provide the evidence that allows accreditation criteria and quality indicators to be defined. Standards and guidelines will also support primary care providers to achieve better quality and outcomes, and can be expected to reduce variation. Finally, publication of standards and guidelines can also serve to professionalise a sector and enhance its standing – particularly important in health systems which are traditionally hospital-centric.

Box 3.5. Defining and promoting the speciality of primary care in Turkey and Japan

Turkey and Japan illustrate well aspects of strengthening primary care. In the former, a central ambition of the *Health Transformation Programme* (HTP) was to strengthen family medicine and primary care. Its reforms sought to reinvigorate the speciality of family medicine (FM), which was first defined in 1983 but failed to embed itself extensively in primary care provision. The HTP 2005 reforms defined the FM core team as comprising a family physician (FP), nurses and professional assistants, to whom a list of named patients was assigned, and who were made responsible for a core set of tasks, focused on maternal and child health. FPs across Turkey are required to deliver a defined set of services, to work to a standard set of norms and are paid according to national terms and conditions, in contrast to the more loosely defined GP which existed earlier. Both absolute numbers of primary care physicians and their distribution has dramatically improved since the implementation of the HTP. Between 2000 and 2008, the primary care workforce expanded from 41.1 doctors per 100 000 to 52.6, and the ratio between the best and least-served areas improved from 8.3:1 to 2.8:1. This was achieved through significant, ear-marked additional investment, with improvement of working conditions and more generous salaries being particularly important. Turkey's primary care/generalist workforce now comprises 33% of all doctors, in line with the OECD average of 30% (OECD, 2014c).

In Japan, very few doctors working in primary care have undertaken specialist training in general practice or family medicine, as is the case in Mexico. Discussions on strengthening primary care, however, have been underway for a number of years. One of the key mechanisms used to drive reform is the national fee-for-service schedule, which applies to both primary and secondary care doctors. Recent additions to the schedule, intended to widen the scope and improve the quality of primary care, include fees to reward the setting up co-ordinated community care plans upon a patient's discharge; to provide information to patients on self-management; to set up cancer care plans; and to provide home care health services. In addition, recent reforms have also introduced a fee if a doctor provides lifestyle advice and co-ordinated management for these patients with two or more of the following conditions: hypertension, diabetes, dyslipidaemia or dementia. Building upon these incremental changes, Japan recently announced that it will establish a distinct and specialist primary care workforce throughout the health care system, as of 2017 (OECD, 2015c).

Some health systems have sought to accelerate this process by importing guidelines developed elsewhere and adapting them to local circumstances. Turkey, in its rapid roll-out of family medicine for example, adopted guidelines developed in Finland (OECD, 2014b). Importing other systems' guidelines is an option that Colombia may wish to consider, particularly for material developed within Latin America. It should be noted, however, that clinicians, managers and patients need to feel a sense of ownership over practice guidelines if they are to be embedded successfully. This is more likely if they have been designed, written and piloted locally, rather than adopted as a finished product from elsewhere. Standards and guidelines can then be used as one of the inputs to develop a curriculum for specialist training in primary care. Development of such a curriculum should be a closely linked priority therefore, both to improve the quality of APS services, as well as enhance its professional standing. As described earlier, Colombia has already taken decisive steps in this direction, with Law 1164 and other initiatives. It will be essential to ensure that new qualifications, linked to the new training programmes, are validated and recognised by EPS and IPS across Colombia, and that work is undertaken so that clinical and managerial colleagues, as well as patients, understand the enhanced skills and roles that the new qualifications bring.

Development and use of the wider primary care workforce, including nurses and pharmacists, should also be addressed. Most OECD health systems are exploring ways in which these, and other, primary care professionals can take on tasks traditionally performed by doctors. In many OECD countries nurses with additional specialist training are undertaking an increasingly wide range of primary care tasks, particularly around chronic disease management, including clinical assessment, ordering investigations, referring for onward care, clinical management and, in some settings, prescribing. The evidence is that extension of nurses' role in this way (supported by an appropriate training, monitoring and governance framework) has not led to any lapses in quality and can be associated with higher rates of patient satisfaction (OECD, 2014a). In Colombia, it appears that nurses have had their sphere of practice *reduced* in recent years, increasingly spending their time on administrative tasks rather than clinical care (ACOFAEN, *Asociación Colombiana de Facultades de Enfermería*, 2009). This trend should be reversed. Colombia should work with professional and patient groups, look to international experiences and explore ways in which the wider primary care workforce can contribute to the country's health care challenges. Legal obstacles to extending nurses' and other professionals' roles should be removed.

Specialist training, enhanced qualifications and accreditation for excellence should be expected to lead to better contracts and reimbursement. As described earlier, primary care doctors in Colombia are employed under contracts of short duration and low pay. This should be addressed. There are plans to improve remuneration and working conditions, and offer scholarships to offset the costs of specialist training. Actual implementation of these plans, however, appears to be at an early stage. It will be important to ensure that actions geared both to the short (for example, more stable employment contracts) and longer term (for example, training scholarships) are taken to make primary care a sought-after speciality. Financial incentives linked to quality and outcomes are one way in which working conditions can be made more attractive at the same time as improving the performance and professional standing of primary care, as discussed earlier.

Innovations in service models should be encouraged, particularly in rural and remote areas

With a clearer picture of the activities, costs and outcomes in APS services, a specialist workforce and enhanced professional standing, Colombia should encourage continued innovation in the delivery models for APS services. The aim must be to provide holistic, continuous, person-centred health care, capable of resolving the majority (90% is the target) of health care needs. As discussed, this will require multidisciplinary working, with teams made up of specialist APS doctors, nurses, pharmacists and wider professionals, working to clear standards and guidelines, and within ambitious accreditation and performance monitoring frameworks.

A priority is to address how APS articulate with other parts of the health care system, and to develop integrated packages and pathways of care for individuals with chronic conditions. Effective co-ordination between APS, public health initiatives and secondary care services is vital to tackle chronic diseases successfully. In Colombia, however, this appears to be inconsistent. The fact that public health and primary care, secondary and tertiary care are provided by public and private institutions according to SR and CR affiliation, creates obstacles for an adequate integration of provision and continuity of care. There are broad system decrees that all providers of individual and population health care services, as well as EPS, unions, academics etc. should work together, but there are few regulations or incentives on the ground to make this happen consistently. Communications between primary and secondary care when a patient is discharged from hospital, for example, are felt to be inadequate, delayed or both.

Defined pathways of care, linked to appropriate standards and indicators, should be developed, with particular emphasis on safety and quality around the transitions of care (for example, upon discharge from hospital). Care co-ordination is an area that all OECD health systems are struggling to define and manage. Some systems have developed successful models that are worth considering, however, such as that in Portugal (see Box 3.6). In addition, an increasing number of standards and metrics around integrated care are emerging, such as unplanned readmission rates (OECD, 2015b). Colombia should consider piloting a select number of these nationally or locally, some of which may be linked to financial incentives. The MSPS should also provide additional support to help EPS, IPS and municipal authorities overcome institutional boundaries and develop more effective operational relationships around health promotion, prevention and early detection. Regionally distributed funds, conditional upon a convincing joint operational plan, or linked to performance targets should be considered. These have been used in the United Kingdom, Sweden, Italy and other OECD countries.

New models of service delivery such as that being developed in Guainía, which is characterised by supply-side investment and community-led design, should be evaluated and, if found to be effective, encouraged. Innovative professional roles should figure prominently in these new service configurations. Encouraging health practitioners such as nurses or pharmacists to take on new tasks has been a key element in meeting rural and remote health care needs, as discussed earlier. Colombia already has a telemedicine strategy in place, and this should be extended to cover more medical conditions and geographical areas. For example, there is potential for telemedicine to link specialists in radiology to rural patients and clinicians. Access can also be enhanced by flying specialists in and out of remote areas. Such schemes work particularly well when a visiting specialist works alongside a local clinician. Outreach specialists should be encouraged to act as mentors to local health care workers, building knowledge and confidence, encouraging continuity of care and, most importantly, forging a sustained service network between rural and urban health care providers.

Box 3.6. Strengthening integrated care in Portugal

Although better co-ordinating patients' care is a focus of policy makers' attention across OECD health systems, it is not often that policy makers can point to real progress in this regard. A typical pattern is for promising local approaches to fail to scale-up to system-wide initiatives that have the potential to transform patients' experience of care. In contrast, Portugal has made real progress, at system-level, in changing the way complex pathways of care are managed.

The introduction of the *Rede Nacional de Cuidados Continuados Integrados* (RNCCI, National Network of Integrated Continuous Care) in 2007 is an example of this. Joint responsibility of the Ministries of Health and of Solidarity, Labour and Social Security, the network sought to better integrate health and social services for the elderly in need of long-term care. Notable features include portability of service users' information across settings (including public and private providers), use of an on-line web-based system allowing the continuous needs assessment and ongoing monitoring of care recipients conditions, and an online data management system (GestCare CCI) that records referrals, admissions, transitions, waiting times for admission, as well as outcomes of needs assessments, with benchmarking of results at national, regional, local and unit level.

More recently, regional adjustment targets have been established to reduce acute hospital care and expand access to long-term care through the RNCCI network. Work has also promoted access to hospital speciality consultations within primary care, agreed local protocols for sharing patients' care between health centres (ACES) and hospitals, and expanded access to teleconsultations, telescreening and telemonitoring to reduce waiting times and offer a more patient-centred service. A particularly noteworthy innovation will be introduction of a unified national referral system. The new system will allow secondary care to book primary care follow-ups upon discharge, for example. Crucially, a episode of care will only be closed and reimbursed once another level of care intervenes to assure continuity of care.

A number of initiatives to better co-ordinate care have also focused on particular patient groups, particularly those with complex long-term conditions. A national programme of integrated disease management was set up in 2009 to improve the quality of care for patients with morbid obesity, pulmonary hypertension, multiple sclerosis and chronic renal failure (chosen because of their prevalence and high cost to the health system). A multifaceted strategy including development of national patient registers with risk stratification, and development of quality indicators with linked pay-for-performance against these was implemented. A database of clinical information and metrics was also developed, and specifically designed to be used equally by patients and clinicians, to encourage self-management. Evaluations of these programmes suggest control of global costs, without compromising quality (Coelho et al., 2014).

These and other new service configurations will need support from appropriate governance and financing mechanisms. Governance can be particularly difficult in remote areas – because of a lack of institutional capacity or poor applicability of levers relied upon elsewhere, such as consumer choice to drive better performance. Nevertheless, quality-focussed governance should be at least as prominent in rural and remote services as elsewhere. More demanding performance frameworks for rural and remote health care services are needed, focussed on population health outcomes. This would involve setting targets based on a mix of local and national priorities, and then monitoring, feeding-back and publishing performance against these. In particular, focussed programmes for forcibly displaced people and other victims of the internal conflict, as well as mental health programmes, should be prioritised in rural and remote areas.

Financing, too, should be tailored to rural and remote needs. In broad terms, Colombia intends to shift to demand-led financing where possible across the health system. This is certainly appropriate where patients are in a position to make an informed choice of EPS/IPS. In rural areas, however, low volumes of patients are likely to make this model of funding infeasible. Instead, capitation- and facility-based funding will be needed. Colombia is implementing this, but more ways need to be found to link this type of funding to outcomes. An element of the performance framework for rural and remote health care services could be to make part of a block grant (or additional funds) conditional upon achieving agreed local or national targets for population health outcomes.

Finally, performance of rural and remote health care services can be strengthened by developing its academic base in Colombia. Innovations such as that in Guainía should be studied by independent bodies, emerging lessons disseminated, and elements of the model replicated elsewhere as appropriate. Colombia should consider developing research and teaching institutes of rural and remote health care, such as exist in Norway and Australia. These offer post-graduate diplomas in this specialised field of health care, as well as lead research in the area. A research institute would also offer the potential of building a richer picture health care needs, service use, quality and outcomes in rural and remote areas.

Box 3.7. Developing the speciality of rural and remote health care in Norway

Norway plays an important role in contributing to international knowledge around the provision of health care in remote areas. One example of this is the Norwegian Centre for Telemedicine based in Tromsø in the far north of the country, which has been a WHO Collaborating Centre for Telemedicine since 2002 (www.telemed.no/home.81328.en.html). The centre aims to research and promote the safe and effective integration of telemedicine services into health care more broadly. Tromsø is also home to the National Centre of Rural Medicine (NCRM, www.nsdm.no/english). NCRM aims to promote education, research and networking amongst physicians and health personnel in rural and remote areas, to contribute to quality improvement and the recruitment and retention of health professionals in rural areas. The University of Bergen also hosts a National Centre for Emergency Primary Health Care (http://uni.no/en/uni-health/). Its focus is on developing the quality of emergency and out-of-hours primary care, by undertaking research and training, setting out standards and maintaining registers that monitor the activity of the out-of-hours services in Norway.

3.6. Conclusions

Recent reforms have made clear the importance of effective primary care in Colombia's strategic vision of how to strengthen universal coverage. A strong primary care sector is seen as central to delivering risk management, early detection and management of health care needs at individual, family and community level, and reducing demand for more complex and costly secondary health services. Colombia has a good base of policies, institutions, financial and informational frameworks in place to deliver this ambition. Several steps should be taken, however, to ensure that the primary care sector can deliver the bigger role being asked of it. Colombia's first priority must be to collect and publish more information on the quality and outcomes achieved by primary care, in order to drive continuous improvement. Transparent benchmarking of quality and outcomes will enhance the status of the sector and assist in developing a specialist primary care workforce, another key priority.

Continued innovation in the models of care, especially in rural and remote areas, is also needed. Differences in the levels of health care resources are still very apparent when comparing provision of primary care in rural and remote areas to urban areas. Differences in population health outcomes are, however, less that might be expected. Nevertheless, it is recognised that a different delivery and financing model is needed in rural and remote areas in order to achieve levels of access and quality that are comparable to more urban settings. Although several initiatives have been introduce to enable this, however, relatively little innovation has taken place on the ground. New models of service delivery such as that being developed in Guainía, should be evaluated and, if found to be effective, encouraged. These and other new service configurations will need support from appropriate governance and financing mechanisms. Quality-focussed governance should be strengthened in rural and remote services, and its academic base developed by creating research and teaching institutes focussed on rural and remote health care.

Note

1. http://calidadensalud.minsalud.gov.co/, accessed 2nd June, 2015.

References

OECD (2015a), *OECD Health Statistics 2015*, http://dx.doi.org/10.1787/health-data-en.

OECD (2015b), *OECD Reviews of Health Care Quality: Portugal – Raising Standards*, OECD Publishing, Paris, http://dx.doi.org/10.1787/9789264225985-en.

OECD (2015c), *OECD Reviews of Health Care Quality: Japan – Raising Standards*, OECD Publishing, Paris, http://dx.doi.org/10.1787/9789264225817-en.

OECD (2014a), *OECD Reviews of Health Care Quality: Norway – Raising Standards*, OECD Publishing, Paris, http://dx.doi.org/10.1787/9789264208605-en.

OECD (2014b), *OECD Reviews of Health Care Quality: Turkey – Raising Standards*, OECD Publishing, Paris, http://dx.doi.org/10.1787/9789264202054-en.

OECD (2013a), *OECD Reviews of Health Care Quality: Denmark – Raising Standards*, OECD Publishing, Paris, http://dx.doi.org/10.1787/9789264191136-en.

OECD (2013b), *OECD Reviews of Health Care Quality: Sweden – Raising Standards*, OECD Publishing, Paris, http://dx.doi.org/10.1787/9789264204799-en.

OECD (2012), *OECD Reviews of Health Care Quality: Israel 2012 – Raising Standards*, OECD Publishing, http://dx.doi.org/10.1787/9789264029941-en

Sarmiento Gómez, A. et al. (2005), "Análisis de eficiencia técnica de la red pública de prestadores de servicios dentro del Sistema General de Seguridad Social en Salud", *Archivos de Economía*, No. 298, Departamento Nacional de Planeación, Bogotá.

ORGANISATION FOR ECONOMIC CO-OPERATION AND DEVELOPMENT

The OECD is a unique forum where governments work together to address the economic, social and environmental challenges of globalisation. The OECD is also at the forefront of efforts to understand and to help governments respond to new developments and concerns, such as corporate governance, the information economy and the challenges of an ageing population. The Organisation provides a setting where governments can compare policy experiences, seek answers to common problems, identify good practice and work to co-ordinate domestic and international policies.

The OECD member countries are: Australia, Austria, Belgium, Canada, Chile, the Czech Republic, Denmark, Estonia, Finland, France, Germany, Greece, Hungary, Iceland, Ireland, Israel, Italy, Japan, Korea, Luxembourg, Mexico, the Netherlands, New Zealand, Norway, Poland, Portugal, the Slovak Republic, Slovenia, Spain, Sweden, Switzerland, Turkey, the United Kingdom and the United States. The European Union takes part in the work of the OECD.

OECD Publishing disseminates widely the results of the Organisation's statistics gathering and research on economic, social and environmental issues, as well as the conventions, guidelines and standards agreed by its members.

OECD PUBLISHING, 2, rue André-Pascal, 75775 PARIS CEDEX 16
(81 2015 30 1 P) ISBN 978-92-64-17904-2 – 2015-01

www.ingramcontent.com/pod-product-compliance
Ingram Content Group UK Ltd.
Pitfield, Milton Keynes, MK11 3LW, UK
UKHW051241300926
15471UKWH00015B/1449

9 789264 179042